To granny
Love Cal

Poems From Wales
Edited by Donna Samworth

First published in Great Britain in 2008 by:
Young Writers
Remus House
Coltsfoot Drive
Peterborough
PE2 9JX
Telephone: 01733 890066
Website: www.youngwriters.co.uk

All Rights Reserved

© *Copyright Contributors 2008*

SB ISBN 978-1 84431 674 8

Foreword

Young Writers was established in 1991 and has been passionately devoted to the promotion of reading and writing in children and young adults ever since. The quest continues today. Young Writers remains as committed to the nurturing of poetic and literary talent as ever.

This year's Young Writers competition has proven as vibrant and dynamic as ever and we are delighted to present a showcase of the best poetry from across the UK and in some cases overseas. Each poem has been selected from a wealth of *Little Laureates 2008* entries before ultimately being published in this, our seventeenth primary school poetry series.

Once again, we have been supremely impressed by the overall quality of the entries we have received. The imagination, energy and creativity which has gone into each young writer's entry made choosing the poems a challenging and often difficult but ultimately hugely rewarding task - the general high standard of the work submitted ensured this opportunity to bring their poetry to a larger appreciative audience.

We sincerely hope you are pleased with this final collection and that you will enjoy *Little Laureates 2008 Poems From Wales* for many years to come.

Contents

    Obaayaa Mensah (10)   1

Burry Port Junior School, Burry Port
    Oscar William Robinson (9)   1
    Abbie Rees (11)   2
    Dimitria Williams (11)   2
    Demi Preece (11)   3
    Stefan Gear (10)   3
    Tiffany Adler (9)   4
    Naomi Lane-John (10)   5
    Natasha Dunn (10)   6
    Brady Thomas (10)   6
    Emma Phillips (10)   7
    Siona Nelson (8)   7
    Daniella Dunn (8)   8
    Nikki Lanfear (10)   8
    Jodie Morris (11)   9
    Rhiannon Howells (11)   9
    Saffron Jessie Taylor (10)   9
    Gwenan Nelson (11)   10
    Alannah Davies (11)   10

Bryn Deva School, Connah's Quay
    Lauren Campbell (10)   11
    Conor White (9)   11
    Liam Shaun Crofts (10)   12
    Casey Burke (10)   12
    Billy Dodd (10)   12
    Ashleigh Wright (10)   13
    Natasha Rose Meyrick (9)   13
    Emma Kate Maguire (10)   14

Carreghofa Primary School, Llanymynech
    Nicola Pickup & Felicity Edwards   14
    Rebecca Pritchard & Shannell Burns (11)   15
    Felicity Edwards (10)   16
    Abigail Walker (9) & Rachel Arthur (10)   16

Jack Watkin & George Andrews (11)	17
Ben Hedley (9)	18
Bethan Evans (11)	18
David Lewis-Jones & Gemma Elliott (11)	19
Jack Watkin (11)	20
Emily Haycocks & Rebecca Pritchard (11)	20
Gemma Elliott (11)	21
Ceri Evans (9)	21
Christopher Davies (10)	21
James Mark Ellis (9)	22

Dolfor CP School, Newtown

Karlie Pagett (11)	22
Jessica Morgan (11)	23
Annie Owen (10)	23
Jac Edwards (9)	23
Abigail Foster (10)	24
Grace Powell (8)	24

Hayscastle Primary School, Haverfordwest

Aled Rowlands (8)	24
Ebony Perry (11)	25
Gethin Rowlands (10)	25
Ellinor Larsson (9)	26
Sean Devonald (11)	26
Cade Kingston (9)	26

Hillgrove School, Bangor

Loren Bishop (11)	27
Carys Morgan (10)	28
Alexandra Wright (11)	28
Libby Vipond (11)	29
Trinity Rowlands (8)	29
Sofia Goula (9)	30
Thomas Porter (7)	30
Jordan Lock (8)	31
Johnny Stanley (8)	32
Kieran Bottomley (8)	33
Anjalina Mitra (9)	34
Sophie Russell (9)	35
Eleanor Aspden (10)	36

Llangain Primary School, Carmarthen
    Christina Walters (10)   36
    Megan Davies (9)   37
    Kelly Rand (9)   37

Oakleigh House School, Uplands
    Chad Nolan-Bennett (9)   38
    Lowri Thomas (8)   38
    Ella Haynes (8)   38
    Matthew Silverberg (7)   39
    Ayesha Anderson (8)   39
    Daniel Cook (8)   40
    Kathryn Percy (7)   40
    Amelia Jefford (8)   41
    India Link-Jones (7)   41

Rhos Street School, Ruthin
    Kirsty Roberts (10)   41
    Elin Wynne (10)   42
    James Wynne (10)   42
    Charlie James Butt (10)   43
    Thomas Padmore (10)   43
    Nathan Huw Jones (10)   43
    Misha Ashford (9)   44
    Declan Alexander Gordon-Astbury (9)   44
    Caroline Matischok (10)   45
    Daniel Ben McCloskey (10)   45
    Finn Nelson (9)   46
    Faye Walker (10)   46

Tonysguboriau Primary School, Pontyclun
    Virajit Pahari (11)   47
    Andrew Eaton (10)   47
    Andrew Hunnisett (10)   48
    Christopher Parsons (11)   48
    Chelsea Woolford (11)   49
    Dewi Jones (10)   49
    Holly Sherrington-Price (10)   50
    Ryan Biscocho (10)   50
    Mitchell Binding (10)   51
    Marcus Webb (11)   51

Matthew Griffin (10)	52
Martyn Donovan (11)	52
Kiaran Gammon (7)	52
Toni Russell (10)	53
Paige Sutton (11)	53
Abigail Rees (9)	54
Jordan Bowen (11)	54
Joshua Parsons (10)	55
Jordan Bailey (10)	55
Rhianne Jones (9)	56
Lois Sophie Ferns (9)	56
Louise Hughes (10)	57
Caitlin Rodd (10)	57
Chloe Louise Freeman (9)	58
Neilla Jenkins (7)	58
Lucy Rose McCarthy (10)	59
Joseph Stringfellow (7)	59
Nyomi Bufton (9)	60
Naomi Hodges (7)	60
Danielle Chick (10)	61
Shaun Donovan (9)	61
Sarah Devine (10)	62
Sharayah Tokeley (8)	62
Iwan Evans (10)	63
Shannon Marie Wiggins (8)	63
Seren Fergusson (10)	64
Maia Chappell (8)	64
Correy Chick (8)	65
Jessica Emma Picton (10)	65
Molly Robson (9)	66
Chloe Chivers (8)	66
Chloe Wesley (10)	67
Nathan Hall (9)	67
Sophie Wiggins (9)	68
Dafydd Lewys Jones (8)	68
Jodie Williams (10)	69
Jacob Hodges (9)	69
Rhys Williams (9)	70
Rachel Ward (8)	70
Jeron Tokeley (9)	71
Caitlin Mead (9)	71
Katie Jenkins (9)	72

Alex Davies (9)	72
Nathan Johnson (9)	73
Seren Hemburrow (8)	73
Huw Phillip Jones (9)	74
Nick Battista (9)	74
Declan Dean Patrick (10)	75
Chelsea Callaghan (8)	75
Morgan Louise Jones (8)	76
Jack Ewan Feist (9)	76
Michael David Bacchetta (9)	77
Ben Robson (8)	77
Thomas James William Herbert (9)	77
Millie Smith (9)	78

Y Bont Faen Primary School, Cowbridge

Charlotte Bonney (8)	78
Molly Gambling (8)	78
Iestyn Thomas (8)	79
Ryan Williams (8)	79
Esme Freeman (7)	79
Siân Prichard (7)	79
Eleanor Howes (8)	80
Bethan Clark (8)	80
Anna Harding (8)	81

Ynystawe Primary School, Ynystawe

Molly Quigley (7)	81
Maddie Cornelius (8)	81
Nicholas Thomas (8)	82
Gwen Crabb (8)	82
Emily Jones (8)	82
Rhiannon Duffy (8)	83
Leah Sell (8)	83
Claire Parker (8)	83
Matthew Blake (8)	84
Luke Thomas (8)	84
Ruth Harry (8)	84
Lydia Jenkins (10)	85
Charlotte Elizabeth Cornelius (11)	85
Jessica Hayden (10)	85

Shauna Hill (10)	86
Jay Thomas (9)	86
Chloe Hill (9)	86

Ysgol Y Foel, Mold

George Cyril Reid (10)	87
Melissa Kennedy (10)	87
Ella Jane Raw (11)	87
Jay Keegan (11)	88
Morgan Nancarrow (9)	88
Hannah Leitch (9)	88
Angharad Williams (9)	89

Ysgol Gynradd Aberporth, Cardigan

Calum James Harry Voller (11)	89
Daniel Mitchell (11)	90
Lauren Louise Chelesea King (10)	90
Samuel Herbert (11)	90
Tomos Wilson (10)	91
Gwyneth Matthews (11)	91
Callum Davies (11)	91
Paul Ryland Dray (10)	92
Daniel George Harries (11)	92
Kelly Davies (10)	92
Amy Kate Lewis (10)	93
Ethan John Nicholas (10)	93
Kayleigh Layton (10)	93

Ysgol Gynradd Mydroilyn, Lampeter

Sammy Boswell (10)	94
Tyler Fice (10)	94
Gabriella Wilton-Baker (8)	94
Chloe Chetwynd (11)	95
Declan Jenkins (8)	95

Ysgol Gynradd Wirfoddol Myfenydd, Aberystwyth

Catryn Davies (8)	95
Thomas Rees-Jones (9)	96
Kieron Owen (9)	96
Sam Robinson (8)	97

Angharad James (9)	97
Rhian Davies (10)	98
Gethin Hughes (8)	98
Ross Diamond (8)	99
Owyn Davies (10)	99
Rowan Hopkinson (10)	100
Caryl Morris (8)	100
Sophie Richards (10)	101
Kingsley Botting (9)	101
Gethin Lewis (10)	102
Jack Davies (7)	102
Bethany Schofield (10)	103
Vickie Hucks (7)	103
Dewi Davies (8)	104
Georgina Williams (10)	104
Lindsey Bassom (8)	105
Sion Hughes (10)	105
Megan Jones (8)	106
Ryan Morris (11)	106
Connie Atkin (11)	107
Hywel Evans (9)	108

Ysgol Heulfan, Gwersyllt

Adrian Howe (10)	108
Danielle Jones (10)	109
Bethan Matthias (8)	109
Liam Jones (8)	110
Antonia Laracombe (7)	110
Courtney Borman (7)	110
Sophie McKevitt (9)	111
Alesha Jones (8)	111
Brandon Manuel (8)	112
Montana Louise Hadley (9)	112
Dylan Edwards (9)	112
Jamie Langford (9)	113
Adam Morris (8)	113
Darren Lewis (9)	114
Leah Roderick (8)	114
Matthew Hughes (7)	115
Nicholas Morris (11)	115
Joe Conway (8)	115

Jordan Luke Edwards (9)	116
Junior Foster-Peprah (8)	116
Leah Dobbins (8)	117
Leah Jones (10)	117

The Poems

The Glittering River

Splish, splosh,
The fish are swimming
Wriggling their tails
As the river is flowing.

Splish, splosh
Watch out!
The kids are throwing stones
And messing about.

Splish, splosh
It's such a hot day
The glittering river
Splashing and splashing day by day.

Splish, splosh
The fish are now sleeping
And the people are in their beds sweetly dreaming.

Obaayaa Mensah (10)

Lightning

Yes, I am Lightning, bigger and stronger
Than any other type of weather.
Dr Run, Master Hailstones, Count Rainula,
You name them and I'm stronger than them.
My arms can reach down to trees and my alarm is my thunder clock.

Oscar William Robinson (9)
Burry Port Junior School, Burry Port

I Am Who I Am, The Wind

I am the wind,
I am the air,
I'm the one
Who touches your hair.

I'm mostly cold
And full of air,
I feel down with
A lot of despair.

All the clouds
Make fun of me,
But really
I don't care

Because I can
Actually touch
Someone's beautiful
Glossy hair!

Abbie Rees (11)
Burry Port Junior School, Burry Port

How The Sun Feels

I am the sun and this is how I feel,
When I wake up, I wake up others too.
I see the horizon; I'm all pink and yellow.
I love all these colours
This makes me feel really great.
It's now midday; I'm up in the sky
Looking down on everyone, some looking at me.
I feel very happy
'Tis night nearly and I'm going to sleep.
This makes me feel very tired and sad
I'm sad because I have to say goodbye.

Dimitria Williams (11)
Burry Port Junior School, Burry Port

I Am The Weather

I am the wind,
I am the air,
I am the one that
Touches your hair.

I am the light,
I am the sun,
I am the one that
Makes you run.

I am the rain,
I am the snow,
I am the one
That knows you know.

I am the sky,
I am the clouds,
I am the one
That booms aloud.

Demi Preece (11)
Burry Port Junior School, Burry Port

The Weather

My dancing raindrops hit the ground,
My clapping thunder boomed out loud,
My whistling wind went shooting,
My gleaming sun shone in the bright blue sky,
My hailstones hurt as they hit my skin,
Hurry up summer, roll on in.

Stefan Gear (10)
Burry Port Junior School, Burry Port

The Four Seasons Of Tiffany

The new animals are being born
And Easter time is coming
Then we'll get ready for Saint David's Day
And we'll dress up pretty.
Some new flowers are growing
So everywhere will be colourful
We'll give cards on Valentine's Day
Because it's a special occasion.

In the summer the clocks go forward
And we'll get our holidays,
I hope we get some sunshine
So I can have some ice cream.
Pools and barbecues out in the garden
Carnivals, fairs, so all the children can play.
If it's hot we can go to the beach,
Picnics, bike rides and play in the street.

Leaves are falling to the ground
It's crisp and golden-brown,
Hallowe'en's scary, dressing up clothes,
Sweets and treats and ghosts around.
Clocks go backwards and a new school year,
Animals get ready for hibernation,
Eat lots and snuggle down
And we get ready for winter.

Christmas time is a family time
It's a short but brilliant day.
Advent begins and the presents arrive,
Cold snow, hats, scarves and gloves.
The frost is shining and the grass feels wet
New Year's Eve party goes with a bang
When Pancake Day comes around
We know spring is on its way.

Tiffany Adler (9)
Burry Port Junior School, Burry Port

What Are Mothers For?

'What are mothers for?'
I asked my teacher one day.
She said to ask her later
After morning play.

'What are mothers for?'
I asked my big sister now.
She said, 'Just go away
I'm trying to pluck my brow?'

'What are mothers for?'
I asked my friend Lizza
She said, 'One minute,
I'm in the middle of my pizza.'

'What are mothers for?'
I asked my big brother.
But he wasn't listening
He was too busy nagging my mother.

'What are mothers for?'
I asked my father.
'Hush up you,' he said,
'I'm phoning Auntie Heather.'

'What are mothers for?'
I am asking myself.
Wait, I think I know.
For keeping up your health!

Naomi Lane-John (10)
Burry Port Junior School, Burry Port

I Am A Snowdrop

I am a snowdrop, clear, cold and crystal-white.
I've waited all winter to fall,
It's finally time,
It's such fun to fall.
I turn, twist and swirl round and round and play with my friends
But I dread the time when I hit the ground and die.

When I woke up
I found myself on the ground with all my friends around me.
I was panicking because I knew the time had come,
But then I did not wake up again!

Natasha Dunn (10)
Burry Port Junior School, Burry Port

A True Liverpool Fan

I am a true Liverpool fan
I always watch them play
I wear their shirt with pride
Nearly every day.

I am a true Liverpool fan
I always want them to win
I hate seeing Gerrard on the bench
Rubbing his injured shin.

I am a true Liverpool fan
And no one can stop me
I want to become a goalie
So they can buy me
And give me lots of money.

Liverpool, Liverpool are so cool
They win some, they lose some
But they are awesome!

Brady Thomas (10)
Burry Port Junior School, Burry Port

Weather

Pembrey, Pembrey
Watcha gonna do
Watcha gonna do
When I come for you?

I've been away, busy all day
Knitting all the clouds into a blanket of grey.

I'll make the trees dance like mad
And lose their leaves so they'll look sad.

Get the lifeboat at the ready
'Cause no one at sea will be steady.

I'll make the floods go up to your door
And make it pour, more and more!

Pembrey, Pembrey,
Watcha gonna do,
Watcha gonna do
Now that I am through?

Emma Phillips (10)
Burry Port Junior School, Burry Port

Butterflies

Butterflies are cute, butterflies are sweet,
Butterflies fly all around me and tickle my feet.
Butterflies are colourful; they fly high up in the sky
But when I look to see them they just wave bye-bye.

Their wings are oh so pretty,
I wish I was a butterfly,
When they fly into the sun
They look like they are having fun.

Butterflies, oh butterflies, please come and play
Butterflies, oh butterflies, please can't you stay?
The night is drawing nearer
I wish I could see you clearer.

Siona Nelson (8)
Burry Port Junior School, Burry Port

My Baby Sister

My baby sister is very sweet,
People say she is so petite.
Kiki is her special name,
Life for her is one big game.
When she throws her food about,
You should hear my mother shout!

In the morning, when she wakes,
You should hear the noise she makes!
She can wake the whole house up,
Squealing like a little pup.
Waiting for her food to come,
Filling up her little tum.

She plays with her toys the whole day long,
Sometimes trying to sing a song.
Even though she can't walk yet,
She follows us just like a pet.
When she goes to bed at night
Kiki puts up quite a fight!

Daniella Dunn (8)
Burry Port Junior School, Burry Port

A Poem On The Weather

I howl like a wolf and I can be quite chilly,
I am so strong, you cannot beat me.
If you try, I will knock you down
And that really is a worry.
I have no eyes, nose or mouth
But I can blow much stronger than you
I hope you like me.

Nikki Lanfear (10)
Burry Port Junior School, Burry Port

The Sun

I am sunny and also funny,
I shine so bright like a massive light.
My face is a ball of fire as I get higher and higher.
As days go by, I sit here in the sky.
Oh, I have no fear as I wait for the moon to appear.
Here comes the moon, I'll have to see you soon.

Jodie Morris (11)
Burry Port Junior School, Burry Port

Ice

I'm lying here in the freezing cold
My lips are blue and bold.
My hair is as grey as can be
The white soft snow is falling on me.

Here comes the sun
That means no more of me, no more fun.
It used to be hi
But now it is bye!

Rhiannon Howells (11)
Burry Port Junior School, Burry Port

My Sister

I have a sister Poppy, with really ginger hair,
She's small and sweet, with tiny feet and freckles everywhere.
She's really very pretty, with big blue eyes as well,
But if she doesn't get her way, she kicks and screams and yells.
My baby sister Poppy, she's small and loud and bold,
Although she shouts and screams a lot, I'll be with her till I'm old.

Saffron Jessie Taylor (10)
Burry Port Junior School, Burry Port

Weather

Rain, rain,
Falls on the street.
Mud in puddles
Splashes my feet.

Thunder, thunder,
Rumble and roar.
Shut all windows
Lock all doors.

Clouds, clouds,
Black and grey.
Heavy with water
They'll drip all day.

Sun, sun,
Is breaking through.
Clouds are moving,
The rain has stopped too.

Rainbow, rainbow,
In the sky.
See the colours
They tickle my eyes.

Gwenan Nelson (11)
Burry Port Junior School, Burry Port

Clouds

I'm all white and I never get smelly
But sometimes I'm full of water and I get all dirty
Then after a while I think I'm full inside
I let it all out so I'm white and fluffy.
But today I wonder what I do,
I just stand here all day and watch over you.

Alannah Davies (11)
Burry Port Junior School, Burry Port

My Cat Milly

There once was a kitten called Milly
She was cute but very silly.
Getting into trouble all of the time
But it doesn't matter because she is mine.

Watching her grow up every day
Loving to sleep and loving to play
And when I am asleep in my bed
She curls up with me by my head.

Learning to play with other cats
And when I call her she always comes back.
Now much older, still cute and clever
I'm going to love my cat forever.

Lauren Campbell (10)
Bryn Deva School, Connah's Quay

My Sister

Tantrums over the telly,
'I want my telly on,' she'll shout.
'I don't want my dinner!
I want cereal!' she'll shout
When I'm working hard.
'Play with me,' she'll shout
When walking the dog.
'I want to hold her,' she'll shout.
'Time to go to bed.'
'I'm not tired,' she'll shout
I'll never change her ways though
Because it's my sister I'm on about!

Conor White (9)
Bryn Deva School, Connah's Quay

Fireworks

Rockets lie on the grass, waiting to touch the sky.
Catherine wheels spin round and round feeling dizzy as they spin.
The fireworks go *boom* as they hit the moon.
The fireworks cry as they go *boom, bang* as they explode.
The hands of the fireworks touch the moon as they go up in the air.
They whistle as they go up in the air.
They go *bang* as they explode.
The Catherine wheel has tears dropping down as they go round
                                                            and round.

Liam Shaun Crofts (10)
Bryn Deva School, Connah's Quay

Cocky Cockroach

There's a cockroach in the kitchen
With a back as hard as rock,
He lies behind the toaster
Beneath the ticking clock.
My brother calls him Cocky
He says he lurks each night,
He eats all the bread
And gives Mum a great big fright!

Casey Burke (10)
Bryn Deva School, Connah's Quay

Bonfire Night

Boom! Boom! The colours are in the sky
The children laugh, the babies cry.
The sparkles sizzle and the fireworks fizzle,
The cold wind blows but the fire still grows.
The people say that the fire is too small,
So they get more logs and burn some more.

Billy Dodd (10)
Bryn Deva School, Connah's Quay

The Spell
(Inspired by 'The Witches' Spell' by William Shakespeare)

Double, double, toil and trouble,
Make those children burn and bubble.

Rich man's eyes
And baker's pies.
Chuck in a frog
And the hairs of a dog.
Mouldy old carrots
And the tongues from some parrots.
Whales' blubber
And pigs' flubber.

Double, double, toil and trouble,
Make those children burn and bubble.

Rebecca's liver
And an old man's shiver.
Shannell's toes
And Bethan's nose.
Emily's blood
And disgusting mud.
Mrs Humphrey's teeth
And Mrs Hare's grief.

Double, double, toil and trouble,
Make those children burn and bubble.

Lightning from the weather
And a pigeon's feather.
Sweat from Todd's bed
And some hair off Gemma's head.
A tail from a cat
And the paw of a rat.
David's jaw
And a tiger's claw.

Double, double, toil and trouble,
Make those children burn and bubble.

Rebecca Pritchard & Shannell Burns (11)
Carreghofa Primary School, Llanymynech

The Spell Of Horror
(Inspired by 'The Witches' Spell' by William Shakespeare)

Snake's eye
Rotten apple pie,
Into the cauldron they go.

Tail of dog, tongue of frog,
Water from a smelly bog.

Double, double,
Toil and trouble,
Fire burn and ingredients bubble.

Wing of bat,
Dead man's fat,
Legs of a cat
Ear of a rat.

Double, double,
Toil and trouble
Fire burn and ingredients bubble.

Cool it with snake's blood,
Then the charm is firm and good.

Felicity Edwards (10)
Carreghofa Primary School, Llanymynech

Darkness

Darkness is black like the dark starry sky.
Darkness sounds like people screaming at midnight.
Darkness tastes like spiders trickling down your throat.
Darkness smells like smoke in the midnight air.
Darkness looks like a goth sitting on a wall of blood.
Darkness feels like blood oozing out of my eyes.
Darkness reminds me of the Great Plague.

Abigail Walker (9) & Rachel Arthur (10)
Carreghofa Primary School, Llanymynech

Recipe For A Disaster
(Inspired by 'The Witches' Spell' by William Shakespeare)

Double, double,
Cauldron bubble.
Watch out world
Cos this spells trouble.

Monkey's tooth,
Tail of a whale,
Dragon's heart,
Head of a snail.

Tiger's spine,
Parrot's eye
Feather of a vulture
Flying high.

Double, double,
Cauldron bubble.
Watch out world
Cos this spells trouble.

Cannibal's mind
Camel turned blind
Lion's paw
Crocodile's jaw.

Spider's legs
Baboon's head
All George's blood
And Jack is dead.

Double, double,
Cauldron bubble.
Watch out world
Cos this spells trouble.

Jack Watkin & George Andrews (11)
Carreghofa Primary School, Llanymynech

Darkness

Darkness is the colour black like the evil eyes of a dragon.
It sounds like a wolf howling in the shade of the moonlight.
It tastes like the horrible devil's skin.
It looks like a dark hole that ends with Hell.
It smells foul like a dead monster.
It feels like no one wants you.
Darkness reminds me of the nightmares in my sleep.

Ben Hedley (9)
Carreghofa Primary School, Llanymynech

The Magic Box
(Based on 'Magic Box' by Kit Wright)

I will put in my box . . .
The tropical fish swimming through the water,
The midnight moon on a cold winter's night
And a present for a child in the warm Christmas light.

I will put in my box . . .
The old brown penny that sits on my shelf,
The ring of the golden church bell
And a drip of water that fell in the well.

I will put in my box . . .
The colour of the sunset that is settling down,
A smile from my nan
A shark's sharp tooth
And my golden dog that goes woof.

I will put in my box . . .
The colour of a magical rainbow that comes up in the day,
The white and golden horn of a unicorn's head
And the pillow of my warm snugly bed.

My box is the witch's poem, 'Double, double, toil and trouble'
The black bat's face and the six leg cat.
The box is covered in the fur of a rat.
I will float along in the chocolate flowing river
On the cookie-filled boat in my rainbow-coloured coat.

Bethan Evans (11)
Carreghofa Primary School, Llanymynech

My Poem On A Kitten

My soft fluffy kitten
Lives in a mitten
It loves to chase its tail
To find a little snail.

It likes to run around
To find food on the ground
Its favourite colour is blue
But he does not know who.

He hates little rats
Because they live in hats
But on the floor
He likes to snore.

He loves to run around the hall
Because he is so small
His name is Tom
Only when the light is on.

Tom is always happy
And sometimes very snappy
Sometimes he can be sad
Only when he is not glad.

Emma Kate Maguire (10)
Bryn Deva School, Connah's Quay

Darkness

Darkness reminds me of the colour black.
Darkness sounds like quiet thunder.
Darkness tastes of evil spirits.
Darkness smells like nothing at all.
Darkness looks like a black evil witch.
Darkness feels like you're being followed by a ghost.

Nicola Pickup & Felicity Edwards
Carreghofa Primary School, Llanymyncoh

The Worst Of Friends

I have a cat called Crystal
She's not a friendly sort,
For when you try to stroke her
In your skin her claws get caught.

She is the blackest cat I know
As dark as the midnight skies,
The only part of her to be seen
Are her collar and her shining eyes.

My other pet is a big mad dog
Dylan is his name,
Crystal and him don't get on,
I think you know who's to blame.

He's a chocolate labradoodle
He's a big, tall, hairy mutt,
He's very nice except for one thing
He keeps sticking his nose up your butt.

Ashleigh Wright (10)
Bryn Deva School, Connah's Quay

Charlie, My Snake

Charlie my snake
Doesn't eat cake
But likes to eat mice
And I am sure that if she could talk
She'd say they're very nice.

Charlie my snake
Loves to slither all around
All around the tank
And even on the ground.
And I am sure that if she could talk
She'd say, 'Gosh, I'm tired.'

Natasha Rose Meyrick (9)
Bryn Deva School, Connah's Quay

Witches' Spell
(Inspired by 'The Witches' Spell' by William Shakespeare)

Double, double, toil and trouble
Boiling in the cauldron bubble.

Eye of a bat and deaf dog's fat
All waiting in line to go in the cauldron.
Squirrel's tail and mouldy bread that's stale,
Sheep's wool and horns from a bull,
In the cauldron they go.
Frog's blood and a pile of mud
And five toes and fingers.

Double, double, toil and trouble
Boiling in the cauldron bubble.

Rat's fur
And a cat that goes purr.
Boiling in the cauldron bubble.
Horses' mane
Jack who's in pain.
Monkey's legs
And sweat from Todd's bed
Mrs Humphrey's heart.
And from a tree bark
Fox's ear
That all the animals fear.
David's fingernail and Emily who's gone pale.

Double, double, toil and trouble
Boiling in the cauldron bubble.

Gemma's arm and Rebecca's palm
In goes Man United.
Bethan's foot and burning black soot.
Shannel's hair and bones from a mare.
Rachel's head and a camel that's dead.
Tigers' claws and a rabbit's paw.
Zebra's hoof and a lion's tooth.
Now the charm is ready.

Double, double, toil and trouble
Boiling in the cauldron bubble.

David Lewis-Jones & Gemma Elliott (11)
Carreghofa Primary School, Llanymynech

Darkness

Darkness is black like the night sky.
Darkness sounds like wind brushing across the floor.
Darkness tastes like spiders crawling into your throat.
Darkness smells like dark mud dripping down the walls.
Darkness looks like a black dark hole.
Darkness feels like tigers taking chunks out of your arm.
Darkness reminds me of spiders crawling over you.

Jack Watkin (11)
Carreghofa Primary School, Llanymynech

The Magic Box
(Based on 'Magic Box' by Kit Wright)

I will put in my box . . .
The tropical fish in the wide open seas,
The stars and the moon from the midnight sky
And the fireworks that explode with beautiful colours.

I will put in my box . . .
The dolphins that leap through the breeze in the air,
A chocolate river that flows over my tongue and the rise of the sun.

I will put in my box . . .
The hot sun from the summer and the cold snow from the winter,
A wishing well to bring me gold and the London Eye to see
                                            my beautiful land.

I will put in my box . . .
A teddy bear with love and my family to share my hug,
A puppy to make me smile and a clown to make me laugh
And a sparkle with my happiest tear.

My box is created from silver with sparkles and swirls for decorations.
My box has shells and silk on its lid, the hinges are made from
                                            elephant tusks.
I will float up to the highest mountains and swim through
                                            my chocolate river
I will bathe in the shallows of my tropical sea.

Emily Haycocks & Rebecca Pritchard (11)
Carreghofa Primary School, Llanymynech

Love Poem

Love is the colour pink like a soft marshmallow.
It tastes like a strawberry dream chocolate that melts in your mouth.
It looks like the shape of a heart with an arrow through it.
It feels like a pink cloud full of love inside your heart.
It smells like the scent of a red rose.
It sounds like a soft heartbeat of a baby.
Love reminds me of my warm and caring family.

Gemma Elliott (11)
Carreghofa Primary School, Llanymynech

Sadness

Sadness is a blue and grey cloudy day.
Sadness is a dark volcano exploding.
Sadness is soggy cabbage on my tongue.
Sadness is onions stinging my eyes.
Sadness is a slow beat of a drum.
Sadness is a bad weather day.
It all reminds me of me and my friend falling out.

Ceri Evans (9)
Carreghofa Primary School, Llanymynech

Cars - Haiku

Cars go on the road
Speeding down the motorway
Cars go rushing past.

Christopher Davies (10)
Carreghofa Primary School, Llanymynech

Happiness

Happiness is love in the air.
Happiness is a blue sunny day.
Happiness is a rainbow high in the sky.
Happiness is strawberry ice cream on my tongue.
Happiness is popcorn popping in the microwave.
Happiness is butterflies in my tummy.

James Mark Ellis (9)
Carreghofa Primary School, Llanymynech

My School

I've been in my school since I was eight
And this school is not to hate.
The teachers are friendly
The uniforms are trendy
And I have made lots of mates.

My favourite subject is maths
I also like arts and crafts.
We go out for break
A football we're allowed to take
And we play in our school ground.
Some play tig and some like to sing
And some just do their own thing.

Our class teacher is Mr Edwards
Mrs Davies likes to help
She works with Years 3 and 4
She doesn't like to shout.

Now that is my school
It's one of the best
It definitely beats all the rest!

Karlie Pagett (11)
Dolfor CP School, Newtown

Cats

Cats like to sleep
But also like to play hide-and-seek.
They sleep all day
And hunt all night
So all you mice
Keep out of sight!

Jessica Morgan (11)
Dolfor CP School, Newtown

Dogs

Dogs like to play all day, they bury bones in the ground.
Dogs take your shoes and they bite them to pieces.
Some dogs are very fat, some are thin.
Some dogs are big, some are small.
Some don't have a home and don't even have a bone!
I think dogs are nice.

Annie Owen (10)
Dolfor CP School, Newtown

Drogba

Drogba, Drogba, why do you fall?
Drogba, Drogba, when there's nothing wrong at all!

Drogba, Drogba, stay on your feet,
Aren't you meant to be one of the elite?

Drogba, Drogba, score a goal,
Drogba, Drogba, don't run into the pole!

Jac Edwards (9)
Dolfor CP School, Newtown

Frogs And Toads

Frogs jump
Frogs hop
They swim in ponds all around
Frogs are green and frogs are brown.

Toads walk
Toads hop
You can see them on the ground
Toads are green and toads are brown.

Frogs and toads
Frogs and toads
They are amphibians
And look cool in the pool.

Abigail Foster (10)
Dolfor CP School, Newtown

Football

Football is my favourite sport,
I have lots of fun playing with my friends.
My favourite team is Manchester United,
I have lots of fun watching them.
If they lose I don't mind, I say, 'Better luck next time!'
Even though they hardly ever lose a match.
One day I hope I will meet them live.

Grace Powell (8)
Dolfor CP School, Newtown

My Dream

Dreams are cool,
Dreams can make you scream.
Dreams are scary, spooky and magical.
My dreams are sometimes short, sometimes long
                                      and sometimes funny.

Aled Rowlands (8)
Hayscastle Primary School, Haverfordwest

Dreams

As I closed my eyes and went to sleep
I counted flowers, bees and sheep.
Two minutes later when I was fast asleep
I invited Megan Parry to come over and eat.
We sat down for lunch
And took a great munch
It made a big crunch.
We finished our meal
On plates with seals
Then we went to bed
With pink fluffy pillows under our heads
And that was the end of my dream.

Ebony Perry (11)
Hayscastle Primary School, Haverfordwest

My Dream

I went up to bed and bumped my head.
I had a dream that was as smooth as cream.
Where was I, past, present, future?
Was I floating, flying or sinking?
No, I was falling into nothingness.
Then a cushion . . . oh no!
A monster so scaly I could scream!
I was sad; it was bad, so hairy and mean
Phew! It was gone.
A cute little bunny rabbit instead of its screams
I want to stroke it and it turned into chocolate!
I was about to eat it when I found myself with my teeth in my pillow!

Gethin Rowlands (10)
Hayscastle Primary School, Haverfordwest

Last Night's Dream

Wake up, wake up,
It's morning, morning.
What was your dream?
Well, I was falling, falling.
Next thing I'm flying, flying
Up and over the skies I fly
Then I'm in the sea swimming madly like all fish do.
Then you wake me up cos I'm snoring, snoring.
Next think I know, it's morning, morning.

Ellinor Larsson (9)
Hayscastle Primary School, Haverfordwest

About A Dream

A dream is sometimes sad or maybe bad.
A dream is sometimes a scream or maybe extreme.
A dream is sometimes romantic or maybe frightening.
A dream is sometimes a floating dream, sometimes
                                I'm floating overhead
Then I find myself out of bed!

Sean Devonald (11)
Hayscastle Primary School, Haverfordwest

When I Go To Bed

When I go to bed I feel like I'm dead.
Just floating across the sea
And when I see a flea swimming after me
I dream that I'm back in bed.

And when I'm back in bed
I don't feel like I'm dead
But I'm wide awake
Eating my mum's Christmas cake
And then I'm going to school.

Cade Kingston (9)
Hayscastle Primary School, Haverfordwest

My Family And Friends

First I have my mum and dad
My brother Kurt and there's more to add.
My grandma who has blonde hair
My grandad who doesn't have much hair.
There's also my cute black border collie
My baby cousin who has a dolly.
There's my aunty who's really nice
She has a cat that catches mice.
My other cousin who has lots of money
And my uncle who is really funny.

Now here are all my friends,
They're with me to the end.
Sophie is my best mate,
She's almost never late.
Then there's Lauren T
Who has the same name as me.
Libby has long black hair
And Elin's favourite animal is a bear.
Angus is very small
And Anthony is quite tall.
Scott loves his quad bike
And Katie likes flying her kite.
There's Hannah, Alex and Carys as well
They all like collecting shells.

All my friends and family are filled with glee
Hold on a minute, I forgot about me!

Loren Bishop (11)
Hillgrove School, Bangor

Fairy Tales

The flaming phoenix leaves a fiery trail
Beside the mystic moon that looks so pale.
The unicorns play at the dead of night
While ugly hags begin to fight.
A dryad is the spirit of the tree
And longs to be set free.
A naiad is the spirit of the well
Wonder what they want to tell.
As the big centaurs charge
The Minotaurs start to barge.
As the talking leopard speaks
The witch chases after what she seeks.
You can hear joyful laughter
So everyone else lives happily ever after.

Carys Morgan (10)
Hillgrove School, Bangor

Ellen MacArthur

Tough strong Ellen
Short, brown hair
Red dry suit
Black lifejacket
A world champion
The best female
Sailer in the world
Sails single-handed
Goes all round the world
She's my idol
That's Ellen MacArthur
The best one yet!

Alexandra Wright (11)
Hillgrove School, Bangor

The Creature

At the bottom of my garden the wild creature likes to eat
Ten boxes of stale bread and a side of luscious meat.
Every day we prod it to make it come outside
It dances and it paddles but only at low tide.
We pat it and we stroke it, we do it every day
Hoping and waiting that it will come and play.
It's as long as me and as brown as a log.
The best greatest creature ever, it's my dog!

Libby Vipond (11)
Hillgrove School, Bangor

My Family

My brother's like a mouse
As quiet as can be,
But sometimes very loud
So I have to read.

My mother's like a dream,
She's so beautiful,
She feels so soft
I could cuddle her all day.

My dad's like an elephant
Very loud when he shouts
But I don't mind.

My grandma's like a sloth
She's very sleepy.
My grandad is a reading machine
He reads every day.

Trinity Rowlands (8)
Hillgrove School, Bangor

The Sound Collector At School
(Based on 'The Sound Collector' by Roger McGough)

*'A stranger called this morning
Dressed all in black and grey,
Put every sound into a bag
And carried them away'.*

The children are daydreaming,
The teacher is still screaming.

The clicking of the clocks,
The banging when someone knocks.

The waking noise it makes when someone kicks the ball,
The children shouting loudly in the big school hall.

*'A stranger called this morning
He didn't leave his name,
Left us only silence
Life will never be the same'.*

Sofia Goula (9)
Hillgrove School, Bangor

My Family

My brother's like a workman,
A good, good workman.
My brother likes to work with tools,
He's a really good workman.

My baby brother's like a squirrel,
He isn't mean
Or anything,
He's really nice.

My cousin's like a fighting machine
Cool
He loves Dr Who like I do
And he's got a sister too.

Thomas Porter (7)
Hillgrove School, Bangor

The Sound Collector In The City
(Based on 'The Sound Collector' by Roger McGough)

*'A stranger called this morning
Dressed in black and grey,
Put every sound into a bag
And carried them away'.*

The dripping of the tap,
The music of the radio,
The closing of the pen
The miaowing of the cat.

The closing of the door,
The rolling of the car wheel,
The squeaking of the floor,
The crackling of the fire.

The ringing of the phone,
The banging of the hammer,
The drilling of the drill,
The destruction of the office.

*'A stranger called this morning,
He didn't leave his name.
He left us only silence
Life will never be the same'.*

Jordan Lock (8)
Hillgrove School, Bangor

The Sound Collector At The Waterfall
(Based on 'The Sound Collector' by Roger McGough)

'A stranger called this morning
Dressed all in black and grey,
Put every sound into a bag
And carried them away'.

The splashing of the waterfall,
The plopping of the coins,
The bubbling of the plunge pools
And when the plunge pools join.

The swaying of the wind,
The whirling of the leaves,
The chatting of the group of people,
The laugher they receive.

'A stranger called this morning
He didn't leave his name,
Left us only silence
Life will never be the same'.

Johnny Stanley (8)
Hillgrove School, Bangor

The Sound Collector At The Zoo
(Based on 'The Sound Collector' by Roger McGough)

'A stranger called this morning
Dressed all in black and grey,
Put every sound into a bag
And carried them away'.

The screaming of the chimpanzee,
The hissing of the snake,
The buzzing of the bumblebee
The scraping of the rake.

The splashing of the seals,
The swooping of the bat,
The swishing of the eel
The eeking of the rat.

'A stranger called this morning
He didn't leave his name,
Left us only silence
Life will never be the same'.

Kieran Bottomley (8)
Hillgrove School, Bangor

The Sound Collector On The Road In Kolkata
(Based on 'The Sound Collector' by Roger McGough)

'A stranger called this morning
Dressed all in black and grey,
Put every sound into a bag
And carried them away'.

The people shouting taxis,
The vendors selling their wares,
The music playing full of glee
From the street side fair.

The horns on every vehicle,
The mooing of the cow,
When will there be a miracle?
I'd like the sounds back now.

'A stranger called this morning
He didn't leave his name,
Left us only silence
Life will never be the same'.

Anjalina Mitra (9)
Hillgrove School, Bangor

The Sound Collector In The Classroom
(Based on 'The Sound Collector' by Roger McGough)

*'A stranger called this morning
Dressed all in black and grey,
Put every sound into a bag
And carried them away'.*

The squeaking of the whiteboard pen
As all the children count to ten,
The slamming of the classroom door
As all the books fall on the floor.

The teacher's chair starts squeaking
The children are overheating,
The radiators leaking
The children are all sleeping.

*'A stranger called this morning
He didn't leave his name
Left us only silence
Life will never be the same'.*

Sophie Russell (9)
Hillgrove School, Bangor

The Sound Collector At Tesco
(Based on 'The Sound Collector' by Roger McGough)

'A stranger called this morning
Dressed all in black and grey,
Put every sound into a bag
And carried them away'.

The screech of the car engine
The ticking of the till
The *bing, bang, bong* of the tannoy
The crying baby's ill.

The faint banging of the feet,
The fizzing of the can,
The clacking of the moving pegs,
The noises of the fan.

'A stranger called this morning
He didn't leave his name
Left us only silence
Life will never be the same'.

Eleanor Aspden (10)
Hillgrove School, Bangor

Skateboarding

I like to skateboard all day long,
It gives me such a thrill inside.
It's easy to get your tricks wrong
But luckily, I only hurt my pride.

My hero's name is Tony Hawk
He skates like he can fly.
He doesn't run, he doesn't walk,
He soars right through the sky.

Christina Walters (10)
Llangain Primary School, Carmarthen

Flowers

Flowers are beautiful
All different colours
Lying in their flowerbeds
Looking at the sun
Growing, growing all day long.

Their petals touch
And bees come by
Stealing pollen on their limbs
Making honey - my greatest whim!

Some have smells that make me dream
I'm on the beach playing
And eating ice cream.

My best flowers curl up at night
They shut their petals tight
And in the morning under the sun
They open again, smile and have lots of fun.

Megan Davies (9)
Llangain Primary School, Carmarthen

Under The Sea

Under the sea there are lots of fish
Shiny, plain and spiky.
There are many seaweeds
Green, blue and spiky.
Jellyfish are rather slimy
But are very shiny.
On the shore sits a tiny shell
Waiting for the tide to swell.

Kelly Rand (9)
Llangain Primary School, Carmarthen

My Colour Poem

Yellow is my bike shining in the sun.
Yellow is the sun at midday.
Yellow is the colour of my fish in the fish tank.
Yellow is the leaves, at autumn, on the trees.
Yellow is the sand shining in the sun.
Yellow is yellow and most of all, yellow is my mum's hair.

Chad Nolan-Bennett (9)
Oakleigh House School, Uplands

Fast

I'm in a race and I'm losing
But then I get faster.
As fast as a cheetah
As fast as the sea
As fast as ever.
What's this?
I've won!

Lowri Thomas (8)
Oakleigh House School, Uplands

My Hamster

Running all around
Trying to escape
From his little cage.
He can see all around
Jumping and climbing
Are his favourite things to do.
He is soft when he rolls into a ball.

Ella Haynes (8)
Oakleigh House School, Uplands

My Gran

My gran is so very kind
She picks me up from school
She helps me with my homework
And listens to me read.

She tells me funny stories
About dragons, lions and bears,
She always plays fun games with me
But never ever wins.

She often makes me dinner
Which is always such a treat.
It is usually fish and chips
Which is what I love to eat.

Matthew Silverberg (7)
Oakleigh House School, Uplands

Summer

The majestic waves swaying to and fro
Underneath the yellow hot sun.
The minutes going very slow
Children splashing in the sea and having lots of fun.
Tall grown palm trees moving in the breeze
Shading all the mums
While the dads are surfing.
Everyone's in shorts with sunburnt knees
And barbecues in the sand.
I never want summer to end.

Ayesha Anderson (8)
Oakleigh House School, Uplands

My India Haiku Poem

The stripy tigers
Tiptoeing towards their prey
As sly as can be.

The snowy mountains
Dark and dim against the sky
So cold and freezing.

The sunny beaches
Bright blue waters glistening
People sunbathing.

The sandy desert
The big blustery sandstorms
People sheltering.

Daniel Cook (8)
Oakleigh House School, Uplands

The Mean Cleaner

When I see the Hoover coming
I run a mile and scream
For when the Hoover comes
He is really mean!

I don't like Mr Hoover
His funny food and ways
He puts me off my breakfast
With all the things he says.

You can see inside his tummy
The dust all soft and runny
His neck is long and thin
Now throw him in the bin.

Kathryn Percy (7)
Oakleigh House School, Uplands

The Rugby

The rugby's on tonight
The streets are empty
The bars are full
Screaming inside
Silence outside
The flags are out
The stadium is open
Play, play, play, play on.
The rugby's on tonight, *shhh!*

Amelia Jefford (8)
Oakleigh House School, Uplands

Perfect Ponies

P erfect ponies do exist
O n a pony club day, she never resists
N ot shying, not bucking, not even a neigh
I t makes it such an exciting day
E veryone claps and cheers us round
S uch a star, she's just won me a crown.

India Link-Jones (7)
Oakleigh House School, Uplands

My Dog

She's big, fat and cuddly
With three white paws
She can be quite funny
When she sleeps she snores and snores.

Kirsty Roberts (10)
Rhos Street School, Ruthin

Spring Lambs

At home on our farm
There are some newborn lambs in the barn
They like to dance around and play
They were born only yesterday.

They like to lie down in the sun
They like to run and have fun
There is a lamb
Who is called Sam.

At home on our farm
There are some newborn lambs in the barn
They like to dance around and play
They were born only yesterday.

Elin Wynne (10)
Rhos Street School, Ruthin

Only When . . .
(Based on a Cree Indian poem from the 19th Century)

Only when we recycle more
And realise it's not a chore
The environment will be a better place
It's come to this, it's just the case.

We waste so much, it's such a disgrace
Our rubbish takes up so much space.

Next time you fill the bin
With plastic, paper, glass or tin
Let's be green and set the scene
Allow the world to be fresh and clean.

James Wynne (10)
Rhos Street School, Ruthin

A Poem

This poem is hard to write
Should it be about cowboys and Indians
Or a king and a knight
I have my pencil and paper in hand
I know I'll do it about a brass band
A frog, a dog or even a cat
Shoes, jumper or a top hat
Maybe I'll just write anything down
As long as I don't make the teacher frown.

Charlie James Butt (10)
Rhos Street School, Ruthin

Only When . . .
(Based on a Cree Indian poem from the 19th Century)

Only when the last ice cap has melted
And the last polar bear has disappeared
And the seas rise
Will we realise it will be too late!

Thomas Padmore (10)
Rhos Street School, Ruthin

Boys In Blue

There was a team that played in blue
Sure enough they knew what to do
No dirty tackles, no ref abuse
But lots of goals they had to shoot
On the pitch with heads up high
They'd face the crowd and wave goodbye.

Nathan Huw Jones (10)
Rhos Street School, Ruthin

My Favourite Animal

The big grey elephant
Wanders through the jungle
With his trunk held high
He likes to flap his ears
And wallow in the mud.
He arrives at a water hole
And takes a long slurp.
Then he splashes about
To wash off all the dirt.
I love the grey elephant
He's so big and strong.
I love him very much
And now my poem is done.

Misha Ashford (9)
Rhos Street School, Ruthin

What Can I Do?

When I am bored
What can I do?
Make a go-kart
Or maybe a canoe.

What colours could it be
Black, pink, yellow or green
Or maybe a colour
You've never seen?

Whatever colours that I choose
In a race I will never lose.

When you are bored
What will you do?
Make a go-kart
Or a canoe.

Declan Alexander Gordon-Astbury (9)
Rhos Street School, Ruthin

I Would Call Myself . . .

I would call myself Pat
But that's only if I had a cat.

I would call myself Ben
But I don't have a hen.

I would call myself Sam
But I don't really like jam.

I would call myself Izzy
But I'm not that dizzy.

I would call myself Helen
In fact, yes, I shall call myself Helen
Because I absolutely love melon.

Caroline Matischok (10)
Rhos Street School, Ruthin

My Dream

My dream is to become a footballer
And play the leading role
I want to play at Wembley
And score the winning goal

I want to be the best in the world
And play for all the best teams
I want the fans to chant my name
And have it the same every game.

I want to be the best I can
And work as hard as I possibly can
I want to be the fan's favourite
The only thing I can do is
Score, score all the goals.

Daniel Ben McCloskey (10)
Rhos Street School, Ruthin

Our Trampoline

Our trampoline is a light shade of blue
Before you go on you take off your shoe.
Bounce, bounce, bounce, very, very high
Bounce, bounce, bounce up into the sky
Bounce, flip, bounce, flip
Off goes my hair clip
Bouncing with my best friend Izzy
Goodness gracious I'm feeling dizzy.

There is one thing you need to know
If you bounce too low
You will stub your toe.

Bounce, pop, bounce, pop!
I'd better stop!

Finn Nelson (9)
Rhos Street School, Ruthin

My Weird Dream

I had a weird dream one night
A weird dream it was
I dreamt I fell off the end of the world
And I fell and fell and fell!
I fell right through the stars
And then I landed on Mars.
I saw a bright light and awoke with a fright
I'd fallen off my bed and bumped my head!

Faye Walker (10)
Rhos Street School, Ruthin

The Playground Life

Children arm wrestling and whoever wins they laugh at their opponent.
People moaning about the heat or the cold.
Everyone shouting, heads up in case the ball hits them.
Children looking at the nice cars passing by.
Going on the grass, getting muddy then getting told off.
Sitting on a bench reading or chatting.
Kicking the ball to one another.
Running and running trying to win a race.
Shivering and wearing their coats on.
People munching on their food, sipping their drinks, enjoying it
                                                          very much.
Running around trees trying to get dizzy.
Teachers telling people off for doing the wrong things.
Scoring goals having extraordinary celebrations.
Cops running around trying to get the robbers.
Sending the naughty ones to the wall so they can't get into
                                               any more mischief.
People sweating and puffing after running around madly.
Sometimes it snows; we wear caps, earmuffs, scarves, gloves
                                                       and coats.
Snowball fights trying to get one another.
Building snowmen, snow ladies for young children.

Virajit Pahari (11)
Tonysguboriau Primary School, Pontyclun

Playground

People play arm-wrestling under the shelter
People are shouting loudly
You can hear the cars drifting past
You can see the park from the playground
You can see houses.
You can see a golf course.

Andrew Eaton (10)
Tonysguboriau Primary School, Pontyclun

The Playground

On the playground we play football.
On the playground there is lots of shouting.
On the playground we sit down and talk.
On the playground the weather is sunny and hot.
On the playground there is a footy pitch.
On the playground we see cars driving past.
On the playground we play tag.
On the playground there is lots of shouting.
On the playground the weather is really cold.
On the playground there is a shelter.
On the playground we see a park.
On the playground we play hide-and-seek.

Andrew Hunnisett (10)
Tonysguboriau Primary School, Pontyclun

Playground

Footballs in the air
People play tag
They bring cards in
Laughing and having fun.
Hide-and-seek
Singing and dancing
Rugby players
Football players
People talking very loud
People eating their sweets
Dancing
Catching each other
People going down the field.

Christopher Parsons (11)
Tonysguboriau Primary School, Pontyclun

The Playground Life

Children arm wrestling and whoever wins they laugh at their opponent.
People moaning about the heat or the cold.
Everyone shouting, heads up in case the ball hits them.
Children looking at the nice cars passing by.
Going on the grass, getting muddy then getting told off.
Sitting on a bench reading or chatting.
Kicking the ball to one another.
Running and running trying to win a race.
Shivering and wearing their coats on.
People munching on their food, sipping their drinks, enjoying it
                                                                        very much.
Running around trees trying to get dizzy.
Teachers telling people off for doing the wrong things.
Scoring goals having extraordinary celebrations.
Cops running around trying to get the robbers.
Sending the naughty ones to the wall so they can't get into
                                                                        any more mischief.
People sweating and puffing after running around madly.
Sometimes it snows; we wear caps, earmuffs, scarves, gloves
                                                                        and coats.
Snowball fights trying to get one another.
Building snowmen, snow ladies for young children.

Virajit Pahari (11)
Tonysguboriau Primary School, Pontyclun

Playground

People play arm-wrestling under the shelter
People are shouting loudly
You can hear the cars drifting past
You can see the park from the playground
You can see houses.
You can see a golf course.

Andrew Eaton (10)
Tonysguboriau Primary School, Pontyclun

The Playground

On the playground we play football.
On the playground there is lots of shouting.
On the playground we sit down and talk.
On the playground the weather is sunny and hot.
On the playground there is a footy pitch.
On the playground we see cars driving past.
On the playground we play tag.
On the playground there is lots of shouting.
On the playground the weather is really cold.
On the playground there is a shelter.
On the playground we see a park.
On the playground we play hide-and-seek.

Andrew Hunnisett (10)
Tonysguboriau Primary School, Pontyclun

Playground

Footballs in the air
People play tag
They bring cards in
Laughing and having fun.
Hide-and-seek
Singing and dancing
Rugby players
Football players
People talking very loud
People eating their sweets
Dancing
Catching each other
People going down the field.

Christopher Parsons (11)
Tonysguboriau Primary School, Pontyclun

The Playground Life

You see children everywhere talking and rushing around
Playing fun games like football and hide-and-seek.
There are many loud noises, like cars rushing past and the bell ringing
to come in.
There is lots to look at, like fields and trees and a park just down
the road.
The weather always changes all the time,
First it's rather sunny then the next time it's cloudy and icy cold.
The sights you see are like the fields and forest scenes.
There's lots to do, you couldn't possibly want more.
It's the best school you could have.
People shouting, 'Come on, let's hide behind the bush.'
There are lots of games to play like catch, tag, mob and many
other things.

Chelsea Woolford (11)
Tonysguboriau Primary School, Pontyclun

Playground Life

Big tall trees standing royally in the distance.
Trees swaying from side to side in the stormy howling wind.
Sunlight beaming down out of the pale blue sky.
Cars thundering down the nearby road.
People kicking a football hard into a goal.
Sometimes it is sunny, sometimes it's raining or even snowing but everyone always has fun.
Children yelling to their friends, 'Come over and play.'
Young children crying because they have fallen over.
Moist, bright, squelching, green grass glittering in the boiling hot sun.

Dewi Jones (10)
Tonysguboriau Primary School, Pontyclun

The Spacious Playground

Flowers gently being blown by the soft breeze.
Children wearing bright green uniforms.
The weather is cloudy with patches of sunshine glittering like stars
                                                              in the sky.
Sometimes a clear sky with the echo of a howling wind.
Branches of tall trees swaying in the wind that swirls repeatedly
                                                           round the trunk.
The sound of a football going through the goal and the team cheering.
Rain trickles down, soaking children that play in the rain.
That's what we do in the playground.

Holly Sherrington-Price (10)
Tonysguboriau Primary School, Pontyclun

The Playground

When there's heavy dripping rain you can hear the raindrops hitting
                                                               the ground.
Shining, sparkling spiderwebs discovered by the rain.
Footballs insanely flinging from the ground into the air.
Trees swaying left and right without a single care.
Gale force winds sweeping sand across the floor.
Scorching sunlight and crazy rain.
Wild children chasing others round the playground.
Blackbirds and starlings soaring through the air.
Gloomy dark pewter clouds covering the big blue sky.
Icy winds blowing onto the playground and frost covering the grass.

Ryan Biscocho (10)
Tonysguboriau Primary School, Pontyclun

The Playground

Many people talking about different things in the playground.
The wind's gust swiftly blows through your ears.
Drivers impatiently sound their horns which the lively children hear
                                    in the noisy playground.
'Tag, you're it!' the children bellow as they chase each other around.
The children sweat as the football soars through the air across
                                          the playground.
The children hide desperately in mischievous places.
The leaves fall off the graceful trees and gently drop to the ground.
Hats blow off heads as the wind makes them fly through
                                          the dashing air.
The trees as still as a rock except for the windy gales.

Mitchell Binding (10)
Tonysguboriau Primary School, Pontyclun

Playground Life

In the playground you hear pupils screaming excitedly,
                          people stomping feet like an elephant.
You see lonely benches, trees swishing, kicking footballs powerfully
                                          into the wind.
Aggressive rugby being played, kids tagging their friends.
All in green with white shirts and grey trousers.
A hot day with a bit of wind, it starts to rain, we all go in.
What to do? Just chill out or talk and play and run around.
Games to play, hopscotch and tag, also throw a ball around.
Boys fighting, teacher comes and shouts
A foggy and misty day, rain pouring down and speeding hail.
Jumping high, smashing the ground, a vibration goes all around.

Marcus Webb (11)
Tonysguboriau Primary School, Pontyclun

On The Playground

The hot sun beats down on you as you run around as fast as you can.
Trees swaying in the breeze.
Children are shouting all around.
Cars going past as we're playing.
Children playing run around.
On the playground you use your imagination.
Laughter all around, having fun.
You play games in the playground, children are shouting all round.
I have a snack in the playground.

Matthew Griffin (10)
Tonysguboriau Primary School, Pontyclun

Playground

There are lots of people shouting excitedly in the playground.
There are lovely benches in good condition.
You can play tag.
We wear uniform every day.
Sometimes it is hot and bright.
All you can hear are children laughing wildly.
Playing games like hide-and-seek, you must never ever peek!
Everyone is in green and are fairly clean.

Martyn Donovan (11)
Tonysguboriau Primary School, Pontyclun

My Sense Of Place

I see the park like a playground.
I smell popcorn in the air like buttery toast.
I taste freedom in the air.
I hear the leaves shuffling around.
I touch the bark on the trees like a prickly porcupine.

Kiaran Gammon (7)
Tonysguboriau Primary School, Pontyclun

My Paintbox

Yellow is sand covering the beach
The hot sun like a fireball in the sky
Daffodils swaying in the shimmering breeze
Happiness is a yellow cheerful sight.

Red is blood going around your system
Love is red hearts around you
Roses are the fragrance you love
Anger is a little evil thing called a devil.

Silver is glimmering small stars in the night
Money is as hard as ice
Jewellery is amazing to different people
Luck is the best thing that could happen to you.

Gold is treasure lying at the bottom of the deep sea
Sand is a glittering shining star
Moon is a gigantic lightbulb
Fairy dust is a handful of glitter.

Toni Russell (10)
Tonysguboriau Primary School, Pontyclun

The Playground Fun

You hear cars zooming past.
Sitting down with chatting all around.
Children wearing green, white black, running around.
Red letter is the cool game we play.
Children shouting excitedly all over the place.
Children everywhere talking, playing like at a fair.
Playing fun games with your friends.
Lovely views of mountains up high.
Teachers watch us run around.
It's always cold wherever we go.

Paige Sutton (11)
Tonysguboriau Primary School, Pontyclun

My Paintbox

Blue is like fresh air
Or a pool just cleaned,
Maybe a touch of frost,
Someone feeling sad.

White is like snow at wintertime
Like clouds on a brand new day,
Lovely diamonds polished every night,
Death is white all over the face.

Red is like a mean dragon,
A bright shining sun,
A person mad with anger,
Maybe a burning fire.

Green leaves falling one by one,
Trees blowing in the wind,
Someone jealous, full of shame,
Nature everywhere you go.

Abigail Rees (9)
Tonysguboriau Primary School, Pontyclun

The Playground

People shouting, 'Pass the ball,' as they fly past.
Children whispering their secrets.
The ball shooting into your goal like a rocket.
Everyone looking smart in their uniform.
Children running away saying, 'You can't get me!'
The rain booming down very heavily.
The wind blowing into people's face.
Children showing their fancy tricks.

Jordan Bowen (11)
Tonysguboriau Primary School, Pontyclun

My Paintbox

Red as a ruby glimmering in the sky,
Fire burning in the bright blue sky,
Mars is red beyond the sky,
Welsh rugby tops waving in their glory.

Blue is as dazzling as the beautiful sky,
Sapphires as cool as the sea,
Neptune as blue as the glittering sea,
Ice when it melts in a cool sea.

Green emeralds as bright as grass,
Apples swaying in the trees,
Leaves swirling to the ground,
Grass so beautiful when it starts to grow.

Yellow topaz glowing in the day,
Saturn shining like a star,
Daffodils flowing gently in the breeze,
Sand spreading to the sea.

Joshua Parsons (10)
Tonysguboriau Primary School, Pontyclun

Playground Life

As we are playing the bell goes
Children are chatting
Children's laughter everywhere
Green grass swaying so smoothly
Trees blowing this way and that
Children messing about playing around
Green uniforms all around
It's raining, it's boring in class
Dark and gloomy clouds are above.

Jordan Bailey (10)
Tonysguboriau Primary School, Pontyclun

My Paintbox

Silver is sparkly glitter
And old treasure in a chest,
The gleaming moon and stars
As shiny as a new door handle.

Blue is as great as the wavy sea,
As new as a blue pen.
Blue is a gleaming fish
And as bright as the shimmering sky.

Pink is sweet candyfloss; delicious and pink,
As tall as a pink tulip,
And as watery as runny paint
On a huge doll's house.

White is as fluffy as clouds
And as great as the snow.
The colour of a mountain tiger matches it
Or the hungry snowy polar bear.

Brown is dusty like an old treasure chest
And is the colour of a rotten twig.
As crunchy as a pine cone
Or as rotten as an old shipwreck.

Rhianne Jones (9)
Tonysguboriau Primary School, Pontyclun

India

I ndia is a great place
N ew Delhi is its capital
D elicious spices and curry to try
I n India they have rangoli patterns on the floor
A nd welcome people through their door.

Lois Sophie Ferns (9)
Tonysguboriau Primary School, Pontyclun

My Paintbox

White is a thick sheet of snow lying on the rooftops,
Snowflakes twirling from the grey sky,
Dark clouds blocking up the bright sun,
Pearls rolling inside shells at the bottom of the sea.

Red is like blood pouring out of a fresh cut,
Juicy cherries that drop from a tree,
Tomatoes growing fresh in summer
Red is just like anger.

Grey is like ash burning in the grass,
Smoke twirling and twisting from the top of a rushing bonfire
Or cement to build a house.

Blue is like an ocean swishing and swaying gracefully,
Aquamarine dazzling on a ring,
Tears dropping from sad eyes
Blue is like a shiver shooting around your body.

Louise Hughes (10)
Tonysguboriau Primary School, Pontyclun

My Paintbox

Red warm blood trickling down your arm,
A sharp thorn raging with pain,
Red roses glimmering in the sun,
Golden autumn leaves falling from a high tree,
The shimmering, soft, golden sand swaying in the wind.

Blue is the sapphire
Slapping against the rocks,
The summery sky glistening high above,
Steam dropping down your soggy face.

Yellow is a scorching hot ball of sun,
Buttercups swaying gracefully in the fields,
The stars twinkling in the darkness,
The harvest fields filled with corn.

Caitlin Rodd (10)
Tonysguboriau Primary School, Pontyclun

My Paintbox

Yellow is a happy spirit
Or twinkling stars at night,
Bright scented cheese smelling old,
A huge gleaming sun shining so bright.

Red is Mars and very hot
Or anger in your eyes,
A glowing fire at your side
Or our colour on St David's day.

Blue is a sad spirit
Or freezing cold wind,
The deep blue sea washing the beach
Or pouring rain at night.

Orange is a summer heatwave
Or hot sand boiling in the sun,
A ripe orange rolling around
Or a person very tanned.

Chloe Louise Freeman (9)
Tonysguboriau Primary School, Pontyclun

My Sense Of Place

I see people walking in the park walking their dogs
It's like woolly sheep in a farm.
I smell the thick grass waving about
It's like the sea crashing on the shore.
I taste the flickering smoke
It's like a puffy cloud drifting by.
I hear the birds chirping
It's like an alarm beeping.
I touch the bin,
It feels as smooth as a woolly sheep.

Neilla Jenkins (7)
Tonysguboriau Primary School, Pontyclun

My Paintbox

Red is like scarlet blood meandering through your body
Or Mars, rocky and hot.
Love hearts and big kisses
And Welsh rugby tops.

Yellow is like soft sand sinking under your feet,
Raging flames of fire,
The brightly lit sun,
Happiness making you laugh and smile

Blue is like the salty deep sea
Or tiny freezing Pluto.
Gleaming, sparkling sapphires shining beautifully,
The bright blue sky giving us light.

Green is like a bunch of fresh, new, juicy grapes
And glimmering, shimmering emeralds
Or the leaves swaying in the tall trees
Turning green when you feel sick.

Gold is like sweet, tasty golden syrup
Or a sparkling new pound coin.
The colour of very expensive jewellery
And glittering, dazzling stars shining brilliantly.

Lucy Rose McCarthy (10)
Tonysguboriau Primary School, Pontyclun

My Sense Of Place

I see the barn like a block standing there.
I smell rubber like a squidgy pillow.
I taste heat like the world expanding.
I hear children talking secrets.
I touch the wind like a tornado.

Joseph Stringfellow (7)
Tonysguboriau Primary School, Pontyclun

My Paintbox

Blue makes freshness.
Sapphires twinkling bright and true
Fighting for warmth against winter blues,
Blue might be Uranus in space.

White is fluffy clouds travelling the world
Little woolly lambs at play.
Snow has fallen from the sky,
Snowdonia is so white.

Gold makes brightness
Or even fairy dust.
It could be hope
Or maybe the rays of the sun.

Yellow is happiness.
A gleaming summer sunshine,
A stream of yellow hair
Or maybe a twinkling star.

Red is the colour of sunset.
Veins carrying blood,
The colour of an English book,
The petals of a poppy.

Nyomi Bufton (9)
Tonysguboriau Primary School, Pontyclun

My Sense Of Place

I see a park but nobody's playing in it.
I smell grass that's been cut.
I taste the wind blowing into my mouth.
I hear noisy cars that make me jump.
I touch a big prickly tree.

Naomi Hodges (7)
Tonysguboriau Primary School, Pontyclun

My Paintbox

Blue is angry waves shouting at the sea.
A lovely blue car shining in the sun,
As cool as a pool on a hot summer's day,
A glittering sapphire shining at the sun.

Gold jewellery shining everywhere,
As gold as a pound coin,
The glittering sun in the high sky,
A bright pot of gold at the end of a rainbow.

Red as bright as our rugby shirts,
As red as the blood of a dying rabbit,
Red flames burning in a fire,
Red is me when I'm angry.

Yellow is a delicious lemon,
The dazzling sun high in the sky,
As yellow as Saturn in space,
A bunch of bananas swaying in the trees.

Danielle Chick (10)
Tonysguboriau Primary School, Pontyclun

Friends

A friend is like Julian.
A friend like Julian plays with me.
A friend is special to me.
A friend will look after me.
A friend tells funny jokes.
A friend will come to the forest to walk my dog.
A friend sticks up for you.
A friend will never fight you.
A friend will knock for you.

Shaun Donovan (9)
Tonysguboriau Primary School, Pontyclun

My Paintbox

Gold is as shiny as a brand new coin,
A gleaming gold ring with a real diamond,
A gigantic treasure chest shining brightly at the bottom of the ocean.

Blue is a lovely cool pool,
The blue sky dazzling in the sunshine,
A gleaming sapphire in a ring,
A big blue monster wave.

Red is the sign of love.
Our Welsh rugby tops are as red as strawberries.
Blood gushing out of a wound,
Flames bursting out of a scorching fire.

Yellow is a lovely bright daisy,
A gorgeous slice of lemon in your drink,
As bright as Saturn,
A delicious banana sliced up.

Sarah Devine (10)
Tonysguboriau Primary School, Pontyclun

My Sense Of Place

I see mountains like big volcanoes with trees on.
I smell fresh air like swirling winds going around me.
I taste the sun like a burning fireball.
I hear the birds like an alarm beeping.
I touch the wind like a ghost in the trees.

Sharayah Tokeley (8)
Tonysguboriau Primary School, Pontyclun

My Paintbox

Green is an emerald sparkling in the sun,
A giant apple hanging from a tree,
Leaves glittering like jewels in the sun
And the scent of the sweet cut grass.

Yellow can be a glittering topaz in the bright light of the sun
Or maybe a daffodil growing taller and taller,
A bright sandy beach with lots of people,
It could even be Saturn high up in the sky.

Blue is the sky shining above our heads,
A gleaming sapphire shimmering in the moonlight,
Neptune floating slowly above us
Or our favourite pair of jeans.

Red can be used for a ruby,
A furious fire burning up
The Welsh rugby top floating in the wind.
It could even be Mars looking very jagged with all its rocks.

Black is dark and has no light.
It's like evil staring at you in the face,
Maybe the night taking over the day
Or even space endless in length.

Iwan Evans (10)
Tonysguboriau Primary School, Pontyclun

India

I ndia is full of beautiful bright colours
N ew Delhi is the capital
D olphins jumping up in the air, in the Arabian Sea
I t's hot
A nd the beaches are paradise.

Shannon Marie Wiggins (8)
Tonysguboriau Primary School, Pontyclun

My Paintbox

Blue is the deepest blue sea,
A beautiful midday sky,
Colour of new fresh bluebells
Or tears dripping down your face.

Green is beautiful spring grass,
Trees swaying in the whistling wind,
Cold enchanting emeralds,
The deepest darkest forest ever.

Yellow lovely sun in the summer,
Enjoyable juicy lemons,
Might be working street lights
Or still the light of the moon.

Red pouring blood which won't stop
Pain hurting so much
Or the Welsh shirt in rugby.
The evil Devil from high above.

Seren Fergusson (10)
Tonysguboriau Primary School, Pontyclun

My Sense Of Place

I see a tree with rustling leaves.
I smell the grass waving from side to side.
I taste the sun shining on my skin.
I hear the rustling leaves on the tree.
I touch the wind that feels cold.

Maia Chappell (8)
Tonysguboriau Primary School, Pontyclun

My Sense Of Place

I see people playing golf like they are ants walking over the grass.
I smell trees like they are blowing up and down.
I taste the green leaves like a jam cake squashed.
I hear cars going past like a volcano is exploding.
I touch the ground; it feels like a prickly leaf falling off the tree.

Correy Chick (8)
Tonysguboriau Primary School, Pontyclun

My Paintbox

Blue is a shimmering sapphire
Or like a breath of fresh air.
Blue is as bright as the ocean
And like the water on Earth.

White is a fluffy cloud drifting along
Shiny glimmering white pearls,
Snow landing on the window
Coming from the sky.

Red is blood pumping around your body
As sweet as a bunch of cherries.
Red means anger
Or a funny clown's nose.

Grey is the colour of smoke,
Cement stuck to the ground.
The fire burns leaving grey ash,
Grey fish swimming in the sea.

Jessica Emma Picton (10)
Tonysguboriau Primary School, Pontyclun

My Paintbox

White could be a fluffy cloud floating in the sky
Or a newborn lamb frolicking across the field.
White snow fallen from a laden tree,
White polar bears, ice-cold from the Antarctica.

Yellow could be glittering gold on the beach
Or shimmering sand in front of the sea.
Yellow is a happy feeling,
It's like a shining sun on a hot day.

Blue could be sad feelings
Or tears running down your face.
Your fingers are blue with cold.
Blue is like the sky, or as blue as the sea.

Red is like juicy strawberries,
It could be pain when you cut yourself.
Red faces when you're angry
Or like the fierce dragon.

Molly Robson (9)
Tonysguboriau Primary School, Pontyclun

India

India has relaxing beaches
New Delhi is the capital
Down in southern Asia
The Arabian Sea is a beautiful blue
Enjoy a lovely curry with rice.

Chloe Chivers (8)
Tonysguboriau Primary School, Pontyclun

My Paintbox

Blue is like a summer sky
With freshness all around.
A pool of tears may arrive
In the cold water.

Gold is like glittering fairy dust
Or twinkling gold tiaras.
Loads of different golden coins
Hiding like they're treasure.

Red is like someone raging with anger
Blood rushing down from a wound
With the sunset gleaming
And the fire burning.

White is like fluffy clouds
Taking shape in the sapphire sky
Little lambs playing about
In the white, white snow.

Chloe Wesley (10)
Tonysguboriau Primary School, Pontyclun

India

I ndia is a really good country
N ew Delhi is their capital
D iamonds, jewels you can buy
I ndian curry and rice
A nd lots of spice!

Nathan Hall (9)
Tonysguboriau Primary School, Pontyclun

My Paintbox

Yellow is the shimmering daffodils in the fields,
And glowing sand on the beach.
The sun is a great gleaming fireball
And happiness is cheerful.

Red is blood pumping in your body.
Love is a beautiful heart.
Anger is a hot volcano just about to explode.
Rubies are red, gleaming and glowing.

Blue is bluebells swaying in the grass,
Water is deep and dark,
Sky is light blue and looks like ice,
The ocean is blue and endless.

Gold is sparkling money,
Treasure is dazzling gold,
Shimmering sand blows on the seashore,
Fairy dust is a sprinkle of glitter.

Sophie Wiggins (9)
Tonysguboriau Primary School, Pontyclun

India

I ndia is in southern Asia
N ew Delhi is the capital
D olphins down in the Arabian Sea
I ndian Ocean, big and strong
A nd people pick crops and really spicy curries.

Dafydd Lewys Jones (8)
Tonysguboriau Primary School, Pontyclun

My Paintbox

Red is horrible pain,
A raw cut dripping from a face,
Blood running from a scared child,
A red ruby placed on a finger.

Gold is a happy, joyful feeling,
A jolly family walking along shimmering sand,
A handsome groom placing a sparkling gold ring on his bride's soft, gentle finger.

Blue is a deep, clean swimming pool,
A crystal sapphire gleaming in the sun,
A hot summer's day, the deep blue sky,
Blue is a pool of tears.

Yellow is the dazzling sun,
Graceful feelings all around,
Buttercups growing from the glorious grass,
Twinkling stars in the moonlight.

Jodie Williams (10)
Tonysguboriau Primary School, Pontyclun

India

I n India there are curry and spices
N ever say no to their lovely rices
D eserted beaches with sparkling oceans
I ndia takes you through millions of emotions
A nyone who goes will want to return.

Jacob Hodges (9)
Tonysguboriau Primary School, Pontyclun

My Paintbox

Blue is like the shining light of the midday sky
Or tears running down your face.
The shimmering deep blue sea
Or as beautiful as a glittering sapphire.

Green is like a deep dark forest in the middle of nowhere
Or monkeys swinging from tree to tree.
Insects scattering across the long grass
Or a magnificent pretty emerald.

Yellow is like an attractive daffodil swaying in the wind
Or like a dim street light in the night.
The moon's light in the pitch dark sky
Or a bright lemon on a tree.

Red is like the Welsh rugby shirt
Or like an evil spirit scaring people away
With pouring blood from a nasty wound.
Red is like burning pain.

Rhys Williams (9)
Tonysguboriau Primary School, Pontyclun

India

India is really cool
And it does really rule.
Rice and curry are really nice
But even better with a little spice.
Ride an elephant around the town
Bathe on the beach, you will never frown.
Meet new people you have never met
Go to New Delhi with me on a jet.

Rachel Ward (8)
Tonysguboriau Primary School, Pontyclun

My Paintbox

Orange is hot burning sand
Glimmering on the beach,
A tanned person sunbathing on the beach
Or a juicy orange in a round fruit bowl.

Blue is a gloomy person bursting into tears,
Freezing cold wind in the Antarctic,
Oceans as cold as freezers,
And a fast man going down a hill.

Yellow is the colour of north gleaming stars
Or bright shining sun,
Plaque stuck to your teeth,
Feeling happy inside.

Brown is the colour of hard splintered wood,
Bare trees swaying in the breeze,
Pure brown nuts falling off a tree,
Children collecting conkers in the forest.

Jeron Tokeley (9)
Tonysguboriau Primary School, Pontyclun

India

I ndia has got relaxing beaches
N ew Delhi is its capital
D own in southern Asia is the Indian Ocean
I n India there is curry, rice and spices
A nd a nice place to relax!

Caitlin Mead (9)
Tonysguboriau Primary School, Pontyclun

My Paintbox

Red is a big explosion
Or maybe a blood-red scar.
A boy going red in the face
Like a bursting firework.

Gold is the sun in the bright blue sky
Or a golden flower dancing in the breeze.
A pool of coins,
A scorching fireball.

Blue is a sapphire sky,
A sparkling sea
Or a bright blue biro pen
And a tear falling from your face.

White is a crinkly cloud swaying in the sky
Or a snowflake falling from the sky,
Snowdrops in a bright field
And white teeth crunching together.

Katie Jenkins (9)
Tonysguboriau Primary School, Pontyclun

India

I ndia is a smashing place
N ew Delhi is the capital
D olphins come up in the morning
I ndia has hot curry and rice
A place where you can ride an elephant
   You can buy beautiful silk saris.

Alex Davies (9)
Tonysguboriau Primary School, Pontyclun

My Paintbox

Yellow is bright sunshine,
It has a happy feeling.
It looks like shimmering sand from a distant view
Glittering like gold on the beach.

Black is a burglar on a scary night
Full of darkness all around,
It looks like murky light.
Black is very cold.

Blue is a sad feeling,
It looks like a deep, dark sea.
Blue is very high in the sky
And it could be tears running down your face.

Red is an angry feeling
It looks like blood from your cut.
Red is a Welsh rugby shirt
And the dragon on our flag.

Nathan Johnson (9)
Tonysguboriau Primary School, Pontyclun

India

I ndia is in Asia
N ew Delhi is the capital
D own in the Indian Ocean
I t is a pretty place
A nd you can have a good time on the beach.

Seren Hemburrow (8)
Tonysguboriau Primary School, Pontyclun

My Paintbox

Red is the planet Mars
Anger, rage and fury.
Red is a glowing fire dancing in the fireplace
Or the Welsh dragon on our flag.

Yellow is the colour of a ripe banana
Or the bright round sun gleaming down on us.
Yellow is plaque on a person's tooth
And happiness in a young boy's soul.

Blue is the deep shining sea
And sadness when something goes wrong.
Blue is the freezing cold wind
Or pouring rain in a rainforest.

Orange is a desert heatwave
Or the hot sand on the beach.
Orange is a ripe satsuma sitting in my fruit bowl
Orange is a very tanned person in the sun.

Huw Phillip Jones (9)
Tonysguboriau Primary School, Pontyclun

India

New Delhi is the capital of India
You can ride up on an elephant,
Eat spicy curry and rice,
A beach on the coast is very nice.
India is in the continent of Asia
Dolphins swim in the Arabian Sea
Crops of rice, pulses and tea.

Nick Battista (9)
Tonysguboriau Primary School, Pontyclun

My Paintbox

Red is a painful scar dripping with blood
Or maybe a ravishing fire burning
Or it could be a massive explosion
Or a huge red planet full of aliens.

Gold is a beautiful star shining bright
Or a pound coin jingling in your pocket
Or it could be the sun gleaming high in the bright sky
Or it might be a lump of gold from a vast treasure chest.

Yellow is a delicious piece of cheese
Or it could be a crescent-shaped banana
Or a furry mane of a lion
Or the soft and silky sand from the sunny beach.

White could be a fluffy cloud in the sky
Or scrumptious white chocolate
Or a ghost hovering in a haunted house
Or snow splattered on the floor.

Declan Dean Patrick (10)
Tonysguboriau Primary School, Pontyclun

Wales

W ales is a pretty place
A ll Welsh people are great
L ots of sheep and shops
E veryone is happy
S heep always sleep in the fields.

Chelsea Callaghan (8)
Tonysguboriau Primary School, Pontyclun

Wales

Sheep graze up on the hills
When you look at the white skies, it gives you the chills.
The miners worked underground
And the mines were full of noise and sound.
People wear leeks and daffodils on St David's Day
And people sing down at Cardiff Bay.
If you look at the mountains, what a lovely sight,
But if you look at the rivers, it's a pool of light.
At the rugby match we all wear red,
We don't cheer for Ireland, we cheer for Wales instead.

Morgan Louise Jones (8)
Tonysguboriau Primary School, Pontyclun

My Paintbox

Black is a monster creeping in the neighbourhood,
Hidden shadows in the night,
Children screaming from the fright,
Monster roaring at the moon.

Red is a fierce fire-breathing dragon,
Hot bubbling lava blasts from the volcano,
The roasting lava burning my skin,
Blazing fires destroying the forest.

Green is a river of slime,
A scary slimy goblin,
A crunchy juicy apple,
A sick little girl.

Blue is a cube of ice in the North Pole,
Fish swimming in the sea,
Sharks scaring children from the sea,
Water glistening like a diamond in the sun.

Jack Ewan Feist (9)
Tonysguboriau Primary School, Pontyclun

Wales

W ales has a capital called Cardiff
A ll the sheep are in the hills
L eeks get worn on St David's Day
E verybody's friends together
S ongs get sung in Cardiff Bay.

Michael David Bacchetta (9)
Tonysguboriau Primary School, Pontyclun

India

On the coast there are nice beaches
Eat hot spicy curry with rice.
Ride wild elephants over the hills
Walk all the way through the fields.
Enjoy shows at night
With the stars shining bright.
The Arabian sea
Is as blue as can be.

Ben Robson (8)
Tonysguboriau Primary School, Pontyclun

India

I ndia is a fabulous country
N ew Delhi is its capital
D olphins swim in the Arabian Sea
I ndian foods like curry and rice
A nd the beaches are nice.

Thomas James William Herbert (9)
Tonysguboriau Primary School, Pontyclun

India

India is full of grace
People love to see this place.
They gather crops and put them in a sack
You can hop on board an elephant's back.
Some of the people in poorer lands
Have to pick crops with their hands.
The beaches stretch far with sand
They're probably the best in the land.
When you go in the sea,
You will think it's the best place to be!
The sun's so hot you could burn
You will leave India wanting to return.

Millie Smith (9)
Tonysguboriau Primary School, Pontyclun

Dylan The Hamster

There once was a hamster called Dylan
Who was a type of villain.
He played on his wheel,
But then had a big meal,
That cheeky little hamster called Dylan.

Charlotte Bonney (8)
Y Bont Faen Primary School, Cowbridge

Autumn

Autumn leaves swirling, twirling up and down
Round and round around the town.
Big ones, small ones, circle and square,
All around in the air.
In fields, gardens, schools and homes,
Lovely leaves.

Molly Gambling (8)
Y Bont Faen Primary School, Cowbridge

Teachers

Teachers are nice and helpful
They shout, they boss and they teach
Teachers take us for PE
Teachers care for children.

Iestyn Thomas (8)
Y Bont Faen Primary School, Cowbridge

Earth

Green, blue,
Reflecting, rotating, shadowy,
Earth is full of life,
Exhilarating.

Ryan Williams (8)
Y Bont Faen Primary School, Cowbridge

James

There once was a boy called James
Who always called me names.
I gave him a slap,
He fell on my lap,
That poor old bully called James.

Esme Freeman (7)
Y Bont Faen Primary School, Cowbridge

My Brother

There once was a boy called Rhys
He had two very big geese.
He jumped on one,
And hurt his thumb,
That unlucky little boy called Rhys.

Siân Prichard (7)
Y Bont Faen Primary School, Cowbridge

Pony Sandy

There once was a pony called Sandy
Who was very handy.
She flew over jumps
And never had bumps
That amazing pony called Sandy.

Her owners name is Ellie
She never ate jelly
She had a friend called Kelly
A nice one too!

Kelly lived in a manor
Oh what a lucky duck
As you can guess, she had a pet
A cute mini Shetland, oh what a pony!

That little Shetland was called Shaggy
Shaggy liked to gallop.

There once was a poem for a lovely little pony
Obviously, perfect
She flies through the air like an angel!

Eleanor Howes (8)
Y Bont Faen Primary School, Cowbridge

Mates

Nice, kind,
Sharing, playing, enjoying,
The best people
Friends.

Caring, thoughtful,
Fun, happy, exciting,
It's very good,
Buddies.

Bethan Clark (8)
Y Bont Faen Primary School, Cowbridge

Teachers

Teachers are nice and helpful
They shout, they boss and they teach
Teachers take us for PE
Teachers care for children.

Iestyn Thomas (8)
Y Bont Faen Primary School, Cowbridge

Earth

Green, blue,
Reflecting, rotating, shadowy,
Earth is full of life,
Exhilarating.

Ryan Williams (8)
Y Bont Faen Primary School, Cowbridge

James

There once was a boy called James
Who always called me names.
I gave him a slap,
He fell on my lap,
That poor old bully called James.

Esme Freeman (7)
Y Bont Faen Primary School, Cowbridge

My Brother

There once was a boy called Rhys
He had two very big geese.
He jumped on one,
And hurt his thumb,
That unlucky little boy called Rhys.

Siân Prichard (7)
Y Bont Faen Primary School, Cowbridge

Pony Sandy

There once was a pony called Sandy
Who was very handy.
She flew over jumps
And never had bumps
That amazing pony called Sandy.

Her owners name is Ellie
She never ate jelly
She had a friend called Kelly
A nice one too!

Kelly lived in a manor
Oh what a lucky duck
As you can guess, she had a pet
A cute mini Shetland, oh what a pony!

That little Shetland was called Shaggy
Shaggy liked to gallop.

There once was a poem for a lovely little pony
Obviously, perfect
She flies through the air like an angel!
Eleanor Howes (8)
Y Bont Faen Primary School, Cowbridge

Mates

Nice, kind,
Sharing, playing, enjoying,
The best people
Friends.

Caring, thoughtful,
Fun, happy, exciting,
It's very good,
Buddies.
Bethan Clark (8)
Y Bont Faen Primary School, Cowbridge

My Teacher

My teacher wears funny clothes
And has freckles all over her nose.
She bosses here, she bosses there,
She mostly bosses everywhere.
And when she can't boss anymore
She'll go right home and lock the door.
Then she lies on the sofa and falls asleep
Before she will do this, she'll have to count sheep.
That's all I'm telling you this fine sunny day,
Don't go to her house just stay away!

Anna Harding (8)
Y Bont Faen Primary School, Cowbridge

Goldfish

It looks like gold.
It feels like silk.
It smells like water.
It sounds like little raindrops falling.
It reminds me of the sea.

Molly Quigley (7)
Ynystawe Primary School, Ynystawe

Love . . .

Love is a red and pink fluffy colour.
Love sounds like soft and gentle fluttering butterflies.
Love tastes like creamy melted chocolate.
Love smells like perfume and roses.
Love looks like pink fluffy clouds and rainbows.
Love feels like a warm sunshine touching my heart.
Love reminds me of happy holidays with the ones I love.

Maddie Cornelius (8)
Ynystawe Primary School, Ynystawe

Sadness

Sadness is the colour of the sky on a wet winter's day, grey and dull.
Sadness is the sound of the moaning wind in the trees.
Sadness is the taste of a bitter lemon, sharp in my mouth.
Sadness is the smell of rotting fruit at autumn time in our orchard.
Sadness is like a wet winter day when you have nothing special to do.
Sadness is the way you feel when one of your family has just died.
Sadness reminds me of a lost crying child looking for its mother.

Nicholas Thomas (8)
Ynystawe Primary School, Ynystawe

Anger

Anger is red like a blazing ball of fire.
Anger sounds like me playing my drum.
Anger tastes like the magic mysterious goblet of fire exploding
 in your mouth.
Anger smells like cheese that has been left in the fridge for a month.
Anger looks like roaring fire.
Anger feels like you're having a heart attack.
Anger reminds me of when The Swans lose.

Gwen Crabb (8)
Ynystawe Primary School, Ynystawe

Fun

Fun, fun, glorious fun
Fun sounds like a thousand giggles.
Fun tastes like sour, sugary sweets.
Fun feels like my heart bursting out with joy.
Fun reminds me of jumping on a colourful rainbow.
Fun is a pantomime full of funniness.

Emily Jones (8)
Ynystawe Primary School, Ynystawe

Fun

Fun is bright yellow like a golden happy sun.
Fun sounds like the seaside when waves swoosh over the beach.
Fun tastes like space dust tingling and popping on my tongue.
Fun smells like summer flowers in full bloom.
Fun looks like a Catherine wheel whizzing and whirring around.
Fun feels like butterfly wings when they dance in the sun.
Fun reminds me of cool splashing water on a hot summer day.

Rhiannon Duffy (8)
Ynystawe Primary School, Ynystawe

Darkness

Darkness is black like the sky at night.
Darkness sounds like a twittering tawny owl.
Darkness tastes like a stick of liquorish.
Darkness smells like a big burning bonfire on Guy Fawkes Night.
Darkness looks like a big lump of coal from the mines.
Darkness feels like a scary haunted house.
Darkness reminds me of the magnificent universe.

Leah Sell (8)
Ynystawe Primary School, Ynystawe

Love

Love is red like a beautiful blooming rose.
Love sounds like your heart beating.
Love tastes like delicious chocolate melting in your mouth.
Love smells like freshly baked bread.
Love looks like my little brother's face looking up at me.
Love feels like a cuddly teddy bear, soft and gentle.
Love reminds me of my family, always there forever.

Claire Parker (8)
Ynystawe Primary School, Ynystawe

Fun

Fun is bright, multicoloured balloons.
Fun sounds like a fairground.
Fun tastes like strawberries and cream.
Fun smells like melted chocolate.
Fun looks like a football match.
Fun feels like you are floating in the sky.
Fun reminds me of jokes and laughter.

Matthew Blake (8)
Ynystawe Primary School, Ynystawe

Fear

Fear is black like a dark scary cave.
Fear is a bang in the middle of the night.
Fear tastes like poison.
Fear is the smell of a damp sewer.
Fear looks like two red eyes looking in through my window.
Fear feels like a cold dry hand grabbing my shoulder.
Fear reminds me of not being able to wake from a terrible dream.

Luke Thomas (8)
Ynystawe Primary School, Ynystawe

Fun!

Fun is the colour of the sun shining on my windowsill.
Fun sounds like the children playing a game with lots of laughter.
Fun tastes like chocolate melting in your mouth.
Fun smells like flowers on a hillside.
Fun looks like my cat playing with a ball of string.
Fun feels like sand going in-between your toes at the seaside.
Fun reminds me of my friend Rhiannon.

Ruth Harry (8)
Ynystawe Primary School, Ynystawe

Fun

Fun sounds like people calling your name to come and play.
Fun tastes like strawberry ice cream.
Fun smells like the seaside breeze.
Fun looks like a million multicoloured balloon floating off into the sky.
Fun feels like a merry-go-round galloping round and round.
Fun reminds me of all my friends.

Lydia Jenkins (10)
Ynystawe Primary School, Ynystawe

Love

Love sounds like some violins playing non-stop.
Love tastes like melted chocolate in your mouth.
Love smells like perfume floating in the air.
Love looks like bright red and pink hearts.
Love feels like someone relaxing in the bath.
Love reminds you of petals drifting in the sky.

Charlotte Elizabeth Cornelius (11)
Ynystawe Primary School, Ynystawe

Love

Love is pink like hearts bursting in your mind.
Love sounds like calm music at a romantic dinner.
It tastes like icing on a warm sweet cake.
It smells like a bunch of roses on Valentine's Day.
It looks like a beautiful Mediterranean island that no one knows about.
It feels like a warm hug from someone special.
It reminds you of two white doves meeting for the first time.

Jessica Hayden (10)
Ynystawe Primary School, Ynystawe

Silence

Silence is the colour of a dazzling cream and white cloud hovering
 in the sky above.
Silence sounds like a bird tweeting in the trees.
Silence tastes like chocolate melting in your mouth.
Silence smells like the autumn breeze.
Silence looks like a rose with white petals.
Silence feels like a butterfly furry and small.
Silence reminds me of my cosy warm bed.

Shauna Hill (10)
Ynystawe Primary School, Ynystawe

Happiness

Happiness tastes like runny chocolate.
Happiness looks like bright red tomatoes.
Happiness sounds like people laughing out loud.
Happiness feels like soft feathers on your face.
Happiness smells like smelly toffee fingers, *yum!*
Happiness is like sweetness.

Jay Thomas (9)
Ynystawe Primary School, Ynystawe

Love

Love reminds me of two people holding hands and loving each other
 forever and ever.
Love tastes like my mum's lasagne.
Love sounds like two little love birds singing a love song.
Love smells like roses.
Love feels like a new day.
Love is the colour red like your heart.

Chloe Hill (9)
Ynystawe Primary School, Ynystawe

The Countryside

The air is clean, the rivers flow gently,
The trees blossom all around,
The gentle breeze blows your hair,
The wildlife, foxes, owls and more,
The cottages and farms,
Those lucky people living in paradise.

George Cyril Reid (10)
Ysgol Y Foel, Mold

My Friend

My birthday is the twelfth
My friend's is the fifth
We play together all the time
And never get miffed.

We go to the beach
We go to the park
We go to Australia but never are apart.

I sleep at hers
She sleeps at mine
We stay up all night and go to bed at nine.

Melissa Kennedy (10)
Ysgol Y Foel, Mold

My Smelly Dog - Haiku

Milly my dog smells
She really does need a bath
Oh Milly smells bad.

Ella Jane Raw (11)
Ysgol Y Foel, Mold

It's Disco Time!

I'm in the disco having a party,
Some men are having a few beers,
I'm standing by the speaker getting hypo and freakier
And the sound is popping my ears.

I'm getting really mad although it's kind of sad
And the beat is beginning to bop,
I'm about to party till I drop
And I really cannot stop!

Jay Keegan (11)
Ysgol Y Foel, Mold

Kangaroo

Kangaroo jumps,
Up to the sky,
Lion cries out,
'The river is nigh!'

Does he listen?
No, he does not!
'Silly old kangaroo,
He's such a clot!'

Morgan Nancarrow (9)
Ysgol Y Foel, Mold

Horses - Haiku

Horses graze on grass.
Riding on them can be fun.
Don't fall off, it hurts!

Hannah Leitch (9)
Ysgol Y Foel, Mold

Spring Lambs - Haiku

Spring lambs are so cute.
They run around when they're born
And they are so small.

Angharad Williams (9)
Ysgol Y Foel, Mold

Bad Hare Day!

My pet hare escaped yesterday,
I'm not sure how!
But he got away,
I couldn't find him, he's not a cow!
Small and stealthy in our house,
Very sly like a mouse.

But on the news one Friday,
We found out where he'd gone.
A man had found him and sold him for little pay,
A scientist gave him a potion, he drank quite a lot.

He was a giant now,
Big, scary and fat!
We gave the scientist a row,
But what use was that?

Our scientist, dear friend,
Concocted some potion for the fiend.
Tomorrow it was,
We used it for the giant hare that reigned
And it worked like a spell from the Wizard of Oz.

After our hare raising adventure,
Our hare was normal pure
And we're happy it was small,
I told my story, I'm really cool!

Calum James Harry Vollor (11)
Ysgol Gynradd Aberporth, Cardigan

My Sister

My sister is blue,
She is a cold winter night
Sitting in the living room.
She is thunder in the sky.
She is a tracksuit bottom
And a sofa.
She is Tracy Beaker
And a big mince pie.

Daniel Mitchell (11)
Ysgol Gynradd Aberporth, Cardigan

My Best Friend

My best friend is yellow.
She is a warm spring day
At the lovely beach.
She is the sun high in the sky.
She is a pair of denim jeans
And a leather sofa.
She is Futurama
And a chocolate bar.

Lauren Louise Chelesea King (10)
Ysgol Gynradd Aberporth, Cardigan

Mrs Morgan

Mrs Morgan is purple.
She is a bright spring morning
On a nature trail on the mountains.
She is a hazy sunrise.
She is a stripy jacket
And a comfy rocking chair.
She is Birdwatch
And a plate of Bara Betws toast.

Samuel Herbert (11)
Ysgol Gynradd Aberporth, Cardigan

Dennis The Menace

Dennis is black and red.
He is a bright summer morning in his tree house.
He is a hurricane.
He is a sweatshirt
And a sofa.
He is a mastermind
And a plate full of cold liver.

Tomos Wilson (10)
Ysgol Gynradd Aberporth, Cardigan

My Horse

My horse is bright green and pink.
He is a warm spring morning
In his cold field.
He is a storm.
He is a woolly jumper
And a comfy sofa.
He is Tracy Beaker
And a carrot.

Gwyneth Matthews (11)
Ysgol Gynradd Aberporth, Cardigan

My Rabbit

My rabbit is white.
He is a summer morning.
He is cold like Alaska.
He is dangerous like a sandstorm.
He is my pillow on my bed.
He is the couch in my living room.
He is Robin Hood
And a carrot.

Callum Davies (11)
Ysgol Gynradd Aberporth, Cardigan

My Dog

My dog is a sweet pink colour.
She is a summer sun in a desert oasis.
She is a distant storm,
She is a woolly jumper
And a cotton chair.
She is 'Rownd a Rownd'
And a plate of stuffing.

Paul Ryland Dray (10)
Ysgol Gynradd Aberporth, Cardigan

My Kitten

My kitten is bright blue,
He is a hot summer morning,
He is a fireplace.
He is a calm sun,
He is a woolly mitten,
He is a small cosy beanbag,
He is Scooby Doo,
He is a chocolate mousse.

Daniel George Harries (11)
Ysgol Gynradd Aberporth, Cardigan

My Brother

My brother is bright orange.
He is a cool autumn day at his workplace.
He is a misty sky.
He is a cold short T-shirt and a cosy bed.
He is Curious George
And is a skinny chip.

Kelly Davies (10)
Ysgol Gynradd Aberporth, Cardigan

My Little Sister

My little sister is red,
She is a bright summer's day.
In her Dora the Explorer bedroom
She is a tornado waiting to strike.
She is a flowery dress
And a comfy sofa.
She is Tracy Beaker
And a fish finger.

Amy Kate Lewis (10)
Ysgol Gynradd Aberporth, Cardigan

My Granny

My granny is pink
She is a hot summer's day
In her living room
She is a warm spring morning
She is a warm fluffy sweatshirt
And a smooth sofa
She is Coronation Street
And a wrinkly tomato.

Ethan John Nicholas (10)
Ysgol Gynradd Aberporth, Cardigan

My Best Friend

My best friend is pink.
She is a warm summer's day
In her cosy living room.
She is a snowstorm above the hills.
She is a pair of scruffy jeans.
She is a cosy sofa.
She is 'Family Guy'.
She is a block of chocolate.

Kayleigh Layton (10)
Ysgol Gynradd Aberporth, Cardigan

I Like . . .

I like having fun
And parties in the sun.
I like going swimming
And doing lots of winning,
But most of all I like to be happy
And sometimes be a little yappy!

Sammy Boswell (10)
Ysgol Gynradd Mydroilyn, Lampeter

My Hamster Scratch

I love my hamster Scratch
She is a devil hamster
Because she bites me
She is a messy hamster
Because there's mess all over the cage
She's a noisy hamster
Because she bites the bars.

Tyler Fice (10)
Ysgol Gynradd Mydroilyn, Lampeter

My Best Friend

I love my best friend Stitches,
She loves me too,
I can't wait to see her face,
It just gleams back through!

I love riding her,
I love grooming her,
But when she works harder,
She gets extra dinner!

Gabriella Wilton-Baker (8)
Ysgol Gynradd Mydroilyn, Lampeter

The World

The world is our desire
There are places where we live
There are countries all around us
Some are small and big
I love this world so look after it please
And keep it nice or
I'll chuck you in the sea.

Chloe Chetwynd (11)
Ysgol Gynradd Mydroilyn, Lampeter

My Kitchen Kettle

My kitchen kettle
is shiny and bright.
You first switch it on
then on comes a light.
The kettle then boils
with water red-hot.
Pour out the water
to Mammy's teapot.

The teapot's a-brim
so who is for tea?
First in the line
I hope it is me.

Declan Jenkins (8)
Ysgol Gynradd Mydroilyn, Lampeter

Winter

W hite winter snow falling from the sky.
I ce skating on the pure white ice.
N ice new woolly clothes keeping me cosy.
T ea nice and warm in front of the fire.
E veryone relaxing for the new year.
R eading a story to each other in front of the fire.

Catryn Davies (8)
Ysgol Gynradd Wirfoddol Myfenydd, Aberystwyth

What Is Yellow?

Yellow is the sun
High in the sky.

Yellow is the moon
Shining brightly above me.

Yellow is the sand
On a sunny beach.

Yellow is popcorn
In the cinema all warm.

Yellow is the daffodil
Blooming in the springtime.

Yellow is calm
On a summer's day.

Yellow is a clarinet
Like music in the air.

Yellow is laughter
Telling lots and lots of jokes.

Yellow is happiness
On a lovely day.

Thomas Rees-Jones (9)
Ysgol Gynradd Wirfoddol Myfenydd, Aberystwyth

Sports

S wimming and winning medals
P ole-vaulting over the high bar
O bstacle course all over the track
R unning for your life to get a gold medal
T eamwork will win you a game of football
S kipping quickly like a boxer.

Kieron Owen (9)
Ysgol Gynradd Wirfoddol Myfenydd, Aberystwyth

What Is Blue?

Blue is blueberries
waiting to be eaten.

Blue is bluebells
in a lovely garden.

Blue is water
in a big pond.

Blue is quiet sounds
in a lonely place.

Blue is feeling ill
coughing and sneezing.

Blue is lonely
having no one to play with.

Sam Robinson (8)
Ysgol Gynradd Wirfoddol Myfenydd, Aberystwyth

What Is Blue?

Blue is the sky
on a summer morning.
Blue is the rain
falling on my head.
Blue is the sea
crashing on the beach.
Blue is the kingfisher
sitting on the riverside.
Blue is the waterfall
rushing to the river.
Blue is sad
when I'm lonely.

Angharad James (9)
Ysgol Gynradd Wirfoddol Myfenydd, Aberystwyth

The Sea

The smooth sea is like a massive world of water
The scary sea snake is like a slippery slide
The baby seal is like a snowflake falling into the sea
The curved sunset is boiling lava

The cold sea is as freezing as ice
The stinging jellyfish has a venomous sting like a scorpion
The blue whale is as huge as our entire school
The angry pirate's skin is as brown as a monkey climbing a tree

The stormy waves are like mysterious tigers pouncing up
The biting shark has teeth like a sharp sharp sword
The peaceful sand is like a smooth blanket waving
The shining starfish is a gold star flickering up in the dark sky

The sucking octopus is like a vacuum cleaner
The little clownfish is like an orange tangerine
The flat hammerhead shark is as fast as a cheetah
The squealing dolphin can jump like a hopping kangaroo.

Rhian Davies (10)
Ysgol Gynradd Wirfoddol Myfenydd, Aberystwyth

What Is Red?

Red is a tomato
Exploding on me
Red is a dragon
Blowing fire
Red is a volcano
Starting to crack
Red is an apple
Ripe on the tree
Red is a rose
In the summertime
Red is my nose
In the winter
Red is blood
Rushing through my mind.

Gethin Hughes (8)
Ysgol Gynradd Wirfoddol Myfenydd, Aberystwyth

Golfing

G olfers getting holes in one.
O ne player gets on the green.
L ift up the flag for the other player.
F ifth hole is a three-shot par.
I an putts it in first.
N o golf balls went in the pond.
G etting ready to play golf.

Ross Diamond (8)
Ysgol Gynradd Wirfoddol Myfenydd, Aberystwyth

I Wish I . . .

I wish I could swim like a vicious shark
Or like a starving bird diving into the wild ocean
I wish I could jump up on the air like excited dolphins
Or explore the bottom of the dark sea floor like a stingray

I wish I could explore the enormous Mary Rose
And see the shy marine animals or watching gentle seals play
Like playful puppies in the sea
Or explore slippery slimy eels

I wish I could watch green plants
Swerving slowly in the current
Or watch elephant seals fighting
For a mate and territory

I wish I could look at
Old sea turtles swimming smoothly
And tiny baby sea turtles doing
Acrobatics in the water

I wish I could but it
Will never come true
I can just watch and learn
That's sea life for you.

Owyn Davies (10)
Ysgol Gynradd Wirfoddol Myfenydd, Aberystwyth

The Creatures Of The Sea

Dolphins dance dramatically like dopey dinosaurs
Jolly jellyfish juggle jams like jealous giraffes
Crazy crabs crash queerly like chaotic cars communicating
Powerful pirates pose proudly like puffing pufferfish
Sandy surfers sound as silent as a gentle breeze
A sunset is a colourful rainbow glassing
Turtles terrify trees like a tyrannosaurus rex
Cool clownfish are colourful acrobats swinging
Sea cucumbers are like the silent sea
Annoying anemones are amazing
A shark is a big bulldozer chasing other fish
Whales are as wondrous as waterhogs
A dogfish is a vicious shark tormenting smaller creatures
Sea monsters are big angry diggers crunching and munching
Starfish are like star-shaped toast
I love the sea creatures.

Rowan Hopkinson (10)
Ysgol Gynradd Wirfoddol Myfenydd, Aberystwyth

Rugby

R unning to score a try
U pon the rugby field
G oing to have a penalty
B ut has it gone over the post?
Y elling and shouting at each other, 'We've won!'

Caryl Morris (8)
Ysgol Gynradd Wirfoddol Myfenydd, Aberystwyth

The Ocean

In the deep Mediterranean Ocean
Boats sway like a turning dolphin swimming
Stormy waves swell in the turquoise sea
Balancing surfboarders surfing like a sailing boat swaying
Rough sand dunes

Hard seashells on the seashore
Tickling starfish sticking to the rocks
Sticky jellyfish floating like someone on a trampoline

A sea turtle gliding like seaweed
A stone sinking like an octopus swimming
A dancing sea snake slithering
A pirate's shipwreck sinking in the sea

A pufferfish like a stone crashing
Fish quiet as a shell.

Sophie Richards (10)
Ysgol Gynradd Wirfoddol Myfenydd, Aberystwyth

Shadow

S unshine shining on us - making shadows
H ouses forming enormous shadows
A pple trees creating scary shadows
D arkness making your shadows die
O nly one side of Earth in the sunlight
W ind in your hair - terrifying shadows.

Kingsley Botting (9)
Ysgol Gynradd Wirfoddol Myfenydd, Aberystwyth

The Seaside

Shining, swift, soft wind
Dolphins dancing through the air like a Catherine wheel
Singing, screaming, silly shrimps
Bouncing bulking boats on waves like
Joyful clownfish juggling like lotto balls in the machine
Sparkling shiny treasure
Pouting, puffing pufferfish
Slippery, sludgy, soft sand
Screeching, screaming water whales
Splashing submarines sinking like a popped balloon
Pirates picking fights
Roaring running dogfish
Hammerhead eating hamburgers
Mermaids munching mackerel
Torpedoes blasting to Texas
Splashing splashing scuba diving.

Gethin Lewis (10)
Ysgol Gynradd Wirfoddol Myfenydd, Aberystwyth

What Is Blue?

Blue is a kingfisher
down on the river bank.
Blue is the sky
with the sun shining brightly.
Blue is bluebells
dancing in the wind.
Blue is ink
writing from my pen.
Blue is sad
When I'm feeling ill.

Jack Davies (7)
Ysgol Gynradd Wirfoddol Myfenydd, Aberystwyth

The Ocean

Blustering breeze rippled the surface of the turquoise sea
Golden sand glimmers at the sight of the boiling sun
While tropical fish swim through the cropped shipwrecks below
Delicate dolphins dance delightfully through the misty waves
Take one flick of their tail and vanish
Starfish's scales shimmer at the bottom of the sandy seabed
While talented turtles triumphantly glide gracefully
Submarines search for treasures beyond your dreams
Amazing sharks gnaw their shimmering teeth
Small seashells wash up on the pebbled beach
While everything is still and calm down below
And lastly . . .
When the gorgeous sun is shining
And the clear sea's so calm I think to myself
I love the sea
Next time come along with me.

Bethany Schofield (10)
Ysgol Gynradd Wirfoddol Myfenydd, Aberystwyth

What Is Yellow?

Yellow is the sand
when I go on holiday.
Yellow is corn
ready to eat.
Yellow are the stars
in the night sky.
Yellow is a banana
that monkeys like to eat.
Yellow is summertime.
Lots of sunshine.
Yellow is a daffodil
that grows through the grass.
Yellow is laughter
with your friends.
Yellow is happiness
and having fun.

Vickie Hucks (7)
Ysgol Gynradd Wirfoddol Myfenydd, Aberystwyth

Tractors

T ractors, big and strong, driving through the fields.
R oaring engines, pulling and towing.
A cres of fields - the tractor ploughs through them.
C louds in the sky blocking the driver's view.
T onne, a tractor weighs 4 tonnes.
O il and diesel, nothing will work without them.
R everse, some things are hard to move with a tractor.
S trength is needed to go through muddy fields.

Dewi Davies (8)
Ysgol Gynradd Wirfoddol Myfenydd, Aberystwyth

The Ocean

The ocean is a tremendous water world
So many captivating creatures to be found
Great sunset shining on the rippling sea like a powerful fireball
As feathered seagulls fly in the cloudy sky

Calm water in the summer is like pretty fluttering butterflies
Camouflaged turtles crawling along the golden sand
Admired dolphins jumping out of the turquoise sea
Salty seaweed dance in the amazing ocean

Treasure buried underneath the deep sea
Blue whales as large as freezing icebergs
A rainbowfish is a fantastic spectrum
Shaped seashells stuck on special coral

A sunny day at the seaside is fun
As you play in the water waves you think . . .
The beautiful playground of the sea
Is such a lovely place to be.

Georgina Williams (10)
Ysgol Gynradd Wirfoddol Myfenydd, Aberystwyth

Fear

Fear is red like lava.
It sounds like a dinosaur running towards me.
It tastes like hot sauce burning in my mouth.
It smells like a fish.
It looks like a witch in my face.
It feels like a ghost running up the stairs.

Lindsey Bassom (8)
Ysgol Gynradd Wirfoddol Myfenydd, Aberystwyth

The Sea

The sea is blue like the shiny, clear sky
The sea is as cold as the Antarctic
The sea is as deep as the enormous world
The sea is as dark as the quiet night
Slimy jellyfish is a transparent mushroom
Swimming quickly in the wide ocean
Tiny fish are shiny steels wiggling back and forth
Large starfish is an orange star floating around in circles
Loud penguins are white pieces of paper
Squealing loudly as they waddle
The shiny grey shark swimming speedily
Enormous shark's teeth grinding through the dirty water
Shark's tail pushing through the smelly water
Sharks bashing quietly through the salty sea
White penguins squealing loudly on the floating ice
Strong waves crashing enormously against the rocks
Colourful boats sailing quietly on the calm ocean
White seagulls squawk on the seaside.

Sion Hughes (10)
Ysgol Gynradd Wirfoddol Myfenydd, Aberystwyth

Winter

W hite woolly scarf and gloves keeping me warm.
I cicles hanging on the roof like lovely decorations.
N ew year has come again.
T oys everywhere no where to keep them.
E verybody sitting by the warm fire.
R obins trying to come into the house!

Megan Jones (8)
Ysgol Gynradd Wirfoddol Myfenydd, Aberystwyth

The Ocean

The salty ocean is a wonderful place
It shines in the bright boiling orange of the sea
The joyful children play in the white waves
Like playful dolphins splashing wildly

The enormous waves rise
The fishing boats tip sometimes
In the scorching sunshine it's calm
The adults relaxing on the soft sand

I wish I could dive into it
The delicious, deep, blue ocean
To the bottom to see the ice lollies of the corals
And find some priceless treasure that will make me rich

The creatures I like the most
The chunky starfish sucking like a Hoover
The sharks biting like a teething baby
The squealing dolphins jumping like me on a trampoline

But at the end of the day
I have to go home
I say goodbye to my ocean home
Until tomorrow . . .

Ryan Morris (11)
Ysgol Gynradd Wirfoddol Myfenydd, Aberystwyth

Titanic Wonder

In the cheerless spooky sea
in my dwarf-sized submarine
going through the uncanny water I see
the dreadful wreck left in the marine

Titanic! The story so sad
it makes me grieve for the dead
the terrible, tremendous deed that has made
me so mad, as mad as a lion roaring out his anger in bed

Hazardous sharks very slyly creeping
round the wreck looking for the beautiful
multicoloured fish hiding in the sleeping wreck
is as quiet as a leaf floating so gracefully

I approach the glorious land
of Liverpool harbour on a busy, sunny day
for the holidaymakers of the sand
but I must be going for I work in Liverpool bay

I look down at the rainbow and the clownfish
and think of my relatives that are long lost under
and I feel like I am a detective and wish
my way through the mystery of wonder

Will I find out more?
Will I find someone of knowledge?
Will I look longer?
Will I find out the mystery of Titanic?

Will I find the answers I need?
Will I?

Connie Atkin (11)
Ysgol Gynradd Wirfoddol Myfenydd, Aberystwyth

The Sea

A cracked ship sails on the cold sea
Like a wet fish swimming swiftly
Disturbing storm and noisy lightning destroying the sand
Like a pink jellyfish stinging amazing scuba-divers

Smooth sand sinking in the sea
Nasty sharks eating little fish to have his dinner
Slimy penguin sliding on the ice
Stormy sea swinging smoothly

Wrinkly crabs crawling slowly
Screaming dolphins dancing in the water
Drenched sea snakes slithering quickly
Clapping seals singing nicely

Damp sand standing by the sea
A fluffy cloud moving in the sky
Brave people fishing in the blue sea
Like a squeaking dolphin jumping

Come with me next time!

Hywel Evans (9)
Ysgol Gynradd Wirfoddol Myfenydd, Aberystwyth

Mother

M y mum is loving
O n Sunday I go shopping
T imes with my mum are great
H er perfume is lovely
E verything about my mum is good
R eally good with my mum.

Adrian Howe (10)
Ysgol Heulfan, Gwersyllt

My Dear Mother

M y mother is very sweet
O h I love my mother
T he love she gives is like a circle which never stops
H er heart is huge!
E veryone should have my mother
R eally loving, hugging mother

L ove is very caring and my mother loves me
O h glorious Mother
V ery interesting things she buys me
E verything is good with my mother

M other, Mother, fabulous Mother
E veryone loves their mum!

Danielle Jones (10)
Ysgol Heulfan, Gwersyllt

My Mum

My mum likes flowers.
My mum likes cooking.
My mum likes to sing with me.
My mum likes petals.
My mum likes to feed the dogs.

She takes me to McDonald's.
My mum likes to help me with my homework.
She hoovers.
My mum likes to wash up.
I love my mummy.

Bethan Matthias (8)
Ysgol Heulfan, Gwersyllt

My Mum

Mums are good
Mums are nice
My mum is wonderful
I love my mum
I love you
You're the only one
You are the best in the world
I hate it when you cry
I love you
I wish it was just me and you.

Liam Jones (8)
Ysgol Heulfan, Gwersyllt

My Mum

My mum is tall and happy.
Her favourite colour is green.
She likes holidays and chocolate.
She is a hard worker and friend.
She's helpful and pretty and a chatterbox.

Antonia Laracombe (7)
Ysgol Heulfan, Gwersyllt

My Mum

My mum is the best
She makes me the best
She is kind and happy
When she is happy I am happy
And she is beautiful like me.

Courtney Borman (7)
Ysgol Heulfan, Gwersyllt

Fantastic Journey

If I could have three wishes
My first wish it would be
To find a wooden ship
And sail across the sea.

If I could have three wishes
My second it would be
To journey into space
And set the aliens free.

If I could have three wishes
My third wish it would be
To land on a snowy mountain
I wonder what I'll see.

Sophie McKevitt (9)
Ysgol Heulfan, Gwersyllt

Along The Railway Track

Steaming.
Old train.
Along the track.
Up the mountainside.
Clouds of fluffy grey smoke.
Chugging along carrying all the people.
Travelling fast past the hedges and fields.

Alesha Jones (8)
Ysgol Heulfan, Gwersyllt

Aeroplane

Flying.
Small plane.
On the wind.
Speeding through fluffy clouds.
Soaring faster than flying birds.
Descending slowly through the blue sky.
I land on the soft grass gently.

Brandon Manuel (8)
Ysgol Heulfan, Gwersyllt

My Dad

When the sun is shining you make me smile
When the moon goes down you're in my sleep
When the wind blows your voice I hear
When you go out you always wear your jeans.

Montana Louise Hadley (9)
Ysgol Heulfan, Gwersyllt

Magic Adventure

Sailing.
Blue sea.
Stormy, windy sky.
Where the waves tumble
Through the fluffy white clouds.
Rocky green islands on the horizon.

Dylan Edwards (9)
Ysgol Heulfan, Gwersyllt

My Wishes For Adventure

If I could have three wishes
My first wish it would be
To climb the highest mountain
And run away to be free.

If I could have three wishes
The second I would make
To build a big green boat
That sails on a giant lake.

If I could have three wishes
My last wish it would be
To travel home in a hot air balloon
Just in time for tea.

Jamie Langford (9)
Ysgol Heulfan, Gwersyllt

Excellent Journey

Over the hill
As high as a steeple
Walking in the park
Are lots of people

Along the river
As long as a snake
Sails a boat
As wide as a lake

Down the lane
As busy as town
Riding our bikes
As happy as a clown.

Adam Morris (8)
Ysgol Heulfan, Gwersyllt

Fantastic Journey

Into space
As black as coal
Into Mars
As round as a ball.

Past the tower
As tall as a tree
Through the woods
As scary as me.

Along the path
As straight as a lamp post
Across Spain
As hot as buttered toast.

Darren Lewis (9)
Ysgol Heulfan, Gwersyllt

Amazing Journey

Over the mountain
As wide as a road
We stood there
As good as gold.

Past the caves
As dark as night
There we flew
As high as a kite.

Into the jungle
As green as grass
We spotted a tiger
As bold as brass.

Leah Roderick (8)
Ysgol Heulfan, Gwersyllt

A Journey Through The Sky

Flying.
Blue sky.
Fluffy white clouds.
Looking out to sea.
Birds flying in the air.
I'm excited about this flying adventure.
Lands on a long, straight, concrete runway.

Matthew Hughes (7)
Ysgol Heulfan, Gwersyllt

My Mum

My mum is caring and loving
She always smiles
You can have a laugh with her
She is the best mum in the world.

Nicholas Morris (11)
Ysgol Heulfan, Gwersyllt

Like A Kite

Flying
Soaring along
Like a kite
Floating on the wind
Through the fluffy white clouds
Over the mountains high and wide
Across the deserts so hot
And dry.

Joe Conway (8)
Ysgol Heulfan, Gwersyllt

My Three Wishes

If I could have three wishes
My first wish it would be
To go to buy London town
See the Queen and have some tea.

If I could have three wishes
My second one would be
To travel into darkest space
And see what I could see.

If I could have three wishes
My last one it would be
To sail a magnificent sailing ship
Across the stormy sea.

Jordan Luke Edwards (9)
Ysgol Heulfan, Gwersyllt

A Journey

Around the mountain
As high as a building
Along the path
As far as space.

Across the river
As wide as space
Over the big log
As old as time.

In the building
As new as a toy
Out of school
As busy as work.

Junior Foster-Peprah (8)
Ysgol Heulfan, Gwersyllt

Fantastic Journey

Across the sea
As blue as the sky
Through the woods
As dark as a shadow

Over the mountains
As green as grass
Into space
As quiet as a mouse

Under the tunnel
As noisy as a party
Along the street
As light as the sky.

Leah Dobbins (8)
Ysgol Heulfan, Gwersyllt

My Nan

My nan would always spoil me.
She had a husband and he always loved her
And while my nan would be in a home he would always be alone.
When she was alive she would always be pleased to see us.
Every time we went to see her
She would call us girls boys and boys girls
Because she lost her memory.

Leah Jones (10)
Ysgol Heulfan, Gwersyllt

Young Writers Information

We hope you have enjoyed reading this book - and that you will continue to enjoy it in the coming years.

If you like reading and writing poetry drop us a line, or give us a call, and we'll send you a free information pack.

Alternatively if you would like to order further copies of this book or any of our other titles, then please give us a call or log onto our website at
www.youngwriters.co.uk

**Young Writers Information
Remus House
Coltsfoot Drive
Peterborough
PE2 9JX**

(01733) 890066